Family Walks
around
Bakewell and Castleton

Norman Taylor

HIGH INTEREST · LOW MILEAGE

Scarthin Books of Cromford
Derbyshire
1994

Family Walks Series

The Country Code

Guard against all risk of fire
Fasten all gates
Keep your dogs under proper control
Keep to public paths across farmland
Avoid damaging fences, hedges and walls
Leave no litter
Safeguard water supplies
Make no unnecessary noise
Protect wildlife, plants and trees
Go carefully along country roads
Respect the life of the countryside

Published 1994

Phototypesetting by Paragon Typesetters, Queensferry, Clwyd

Printed by Redwood Books

ISBN 0 907758 70 3

Cover illustration by Andrew Ravenwood: *Peveril Castle, Castleton, and Mam Tor (Route 14)*

Abandoned millstones at Bole Hill (Route 11).

Acknowledgements

In writing this book, I have had help in one form or another from a number of people, and I would like to record my appreciation of their contributions.

First, I must thank Roland Smith of the Peak Park Board, along with those members of the Ranger Service who were involved, for checking the routes.

I would like to thank Geoff Nickolds of Severn Trent Water for information and advice concerning concessionary footpaths in the Upper Derwent, and also David Wilson, C.M. Jones and T.J.G. Crump of the National Trust for their up-to-date information and advice on footpaths in the same area.

I thank the Chatsworth Trustees for permission to direct family walkers across a section of Chatsworth Park that does not have a public right of way.

My thanks are due to Gez Boothby and Ken Wrigley for their suggestions for walks for inclusion to this guide. And thank you also to Gez, Wendy Brown and Tim, and to Pam and Mike West for sampling and checking some of the route descriptions without the accompanying maps — the best way to achieve quality control!

Once again, I must thank my publishers Dave Mitchell and George Power for suggesting that I should compile a new selection of Family Walks in the Peak District.

And, finally, I am indebted to my wife, Sue, for her encouragement and support during the production of this guide, and to our two sons, Matthew and Sam, for taking Family Walks on board.

About the author

Originator and general editor of the Family Walks series, Norman Taylor now has four of these guides to his credit. Brought up as one of four children in a small East Lancashire cotton town, his interest in the outdoors was fired by his parents' enthusiasm for regular family outings to the countryside and the seaside. For the past twenty-two years he has lived and worked in Sheffield, and is married with two sons. It is in the course of his work as a teacher, and because he is a keen climber and walker, that he has developed an intimate knowledge of the Peak District.

Contents

Map of the area

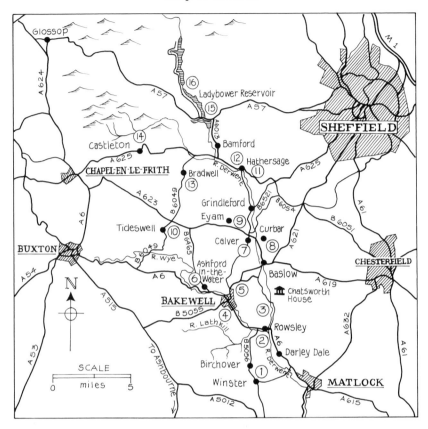

Cowslip. April – May (Yellow)

Introduction

My third Peak District Family Walks guide, this new selection of circular walks embraces both limestone and gritstone Peakland. Starting within six miles of either Bakewell or Castleton, they offer a wide choice both in length and character: from the forests and hills around Ladybower in the north to the former lead-mining country around Winster in the south, and from the dry limestone dales around Tideswell in the west to the gritstone edges and river valleys in the east.

Although there are 16 'Routes', in fact 30 walks are described when all the variations are included, providing a wide choice no matter what the weather, the season, or the stamina of the walking party.

The walks are mainly between 2½ and 6 miles in length, with lots of interest for youngsters and adults alike. But they are not exclusive to families, and many other walkers may find this guide suited to their taste.

The more strenuous parts of each walk are nearly always within the first half, with easier, often downhill walking to complete the journey. Road-walking is kept to a minimum, and where it is unavoidable only short sections are involved.

All the walks have several focal points which break up the journey and are attractive to children, such as streams, woods, ponds and weirs, rocks to scramble on, historical relics to explore, interesting wildlife and good picnic spots. Where possible, the walks happen on a wayside inn or tea-shop around the halfway mark or a little further along.   .

Choosing a walk

Unless the children taking part are seasoned walkers, it is best not to be too ambitious at first; walking along uneven footpaths or scaling a hillside is hard going if you are not used to it. In the case of very young children, start by walking interesting parts of the lower level routes, and even then be prepared to turn back. The aim is to introduce them to the joys of the countryside and not to put them off for ever! And with older children who are newcomers to walking it is advisable to start with the shorter, easier walks and build up gradually to the longer and more strenuous walks.

To help in choosing a walk, I have listed the routes in order of difficulty at the back of the book. This is a subjective judgement but should serve as a useful guide.

Allowing sufficient time

Each walk is intended as the best part of a day's outing, allowing time for play, exploration and rest stops. It is better to overestimate than underestimate the time it may take, and then have to route-march the latter part of the walk. As a rough guide, allow a pace of around one mile per hour for the younger child, graduating to two miles per hour for the experienced 11 year old. Where hill-climbing is involved, add on extra time dependent on the size and stamina of the children in the party.

Clothing

British weather being as unpredictable as it is, I would advise the family walker to go prepared for wet weather. For the grown-ups, a pair of lightweight walking boots are recommended, preferably ones that are waterproof. At the same time, boots provide ankle support along rough terrain and a better grip on slippery footpaths. But children grow out of footwear so quickly, and expensive walking boots are out of the question for most people. As a substitute, trainers are ideal for most conditions if spare socks are carried; even in slightly damp conditions trainers will not keep the feet dry but the spare, dry socks provide the solution. Where muddy or wet conditions are likely for considerable parts of a walk, good fitting wellingtons worn with knee-length hiking socks are best.

Waterproof outer clothes are essential for every member of the party. The cagoule is especially useful since it is also windproof, light and easy to pack in a rucksack. The same goes for overtrousers. If going out in the winter months or onto the hills or 'edges' in dubious weather at other times of year, it is advisable to take spare warm clothing for everyone.

First aid kit

A basic first aid kit should be carried so that the odd cut or emerging blister can be attended to.

Footpaths and rights of way

All the walks in this guide use public rights of way or paths that have been made available for use by the general public. Although in most cases footpaths are well-defined, there are one or two exceptions where, due to infrequent use, the way ahead is less obvious. However, the routes are described in sufficient detail for this not to pose insurmountable problems in route finding.

Except in countryside where there is 'Open Access', which is always clearly indicated on signposts, you should keep to the footpath. This is especially true when crossing farmland. Walkers need the cooperation of farmers and this will only be forthcoming if due respect is shown when crossing their land.

At the same time, there is the odd occasion when a stile or a public right of way has been blocked. In the unlikely event of this happening, use your initiative to get over the obstacle, *avoiding damage to fences and walls*, and report the matter to myself or the Rambler's Association. Where a right of way has been ploughed, you should continue in the direction of the right of way even if this means treading on crops. There are two reasons for this. Firstly, the farmer is required by law to make good the surface of a public footpath subsequent to ploughing or sowing. Secondly, by making a detour around a crop, you are trespassing.

The maps

The maps in this guide, in combination with the route descriptions, are sufficiently detailed to be used without reference to other maps of the area. Many walkers will wish to take the standard OS sheets (1:25000 series) with them, however, and appropriate grid references are given for each route.

Refreshments

For each walk, pubs and tea-shops encountered en route are mentioned. In the case of pubs and inns, a brief description of catering and facilities for those with children is given.

All the pubs and inns mentioned in the guide allow children accompanied by adults into their premises if purchasing pub food. Some of the pubs, however, have 'family' or 'children's' rooms or space out of sight of the bar where children are permitted to sit for drinks. This is shown under 'Refreshments' as 'children admitted'.

Many pubs also have beer gardens or outside seating, and their locations are sufficiently pleasant to drink and relax outside if the weather is good.

On many of the walks, tea-shops are mentioned. As a general rule, these can be relied on to be open during the summer season, although some stay open for most of the year.

Transport to the area

Although I have assumed most people will travel to the area by car, most of the walks can be reached by bus from the larger towns in the Peak District, and many are accessible from Sheffield, Chesterfield, Matlock, Buxton, and Stockport. Brief details are given at the end of route descriptions, and there is a list of relevant bus operators in the Appendices. Also, Derbyshire County Council publish the "Peak District Timetable" of bus and rail services, and this is available from local bus enquiry offices and Tourist Information Offices, or by post from Derbyshire County Council, Public Transport Unit.

Weather Forecast

For an up-to-date forecast of the Peak District, telephone Mountaincall 0839 168 370.

Map Key

Route (right of way unless otherwise stated)		Woods	
Concessionary footpath en route		Lake Pond	
Route (no recognizable footpath)		Hilltop	△
Route variation		Triangulation pillar	△
Footpath *not* en route		Village or hamlet	
Track or drive		Building	■
Road		Church	+
Disused railway ('trail')		Cave	⌒
Crag		Footbridge	
Steep slope		River or stream (showing direction of flow)	
Steep-sided valley or gorge		Stepping stones	ST
		④ etc. Number corresponds with route direction	

10

Climbers on Curbar Edge (Route 8)

Clough Wood and Rowtor Rocks

Outline
Winster − Clough Wood − Birchover − Rowtor Rocks − Upper Town − Winster.

Summary
An excellent walk with plenty of variety on the limestone-gritstone boundary in a quiet corner of the Peak District. Clear footpaths and tracks are followed through the pastures and woodland that lie between the two ancient settlements of Winster and Birchover. There is a lot of wildlife interest, and the relics of a once important lead mine are passed en route. A visit to the unusual and fascinating Rowtor Rocks could be included. After a spell of wet weather, some of the footpaths can be particularly muddy.

Attractions
The walk begins at Winster, a most attractive village of stone-built cottages. Although there are also several interesting larger buildings, the 16th century Market Hall at the centre of the village, now an Information Centre run by the National Trust, deserves more than a passing glance. A closer inspection of some of the old cottages will reveal a mixture of building stone − some of it is gritstone and some limestone. This reflects the geological location of Winster on the limestone-gritstone boundary.

At the time of the Domesday Survey in 1086, Winster had twenty dwellings. It expanded rapidly, however, during the 18th century as a result of the lead mining industry, when there were more than twenty mines operating in the immediate vicinity.

On leaving Winster, the route soon enters a wild stretch of woodland which displays a wide variety of trees, shrubs and wild flowers, amongst which may be found wood anemones, wood violets and field bindweed. The bird life is also rich and varied, and a pair of binoculars would be useful on this walk. As you pass through the woods, you may be lucky enough to spot a roe deer. Failing this, keep an eye out for their tracks along the footpath.

On this section of the walk, various relics from the lead-mining era can be seen. Most notable is the ruined engine house at Cowley Knowl. Adjacent to it is a deep shaft which is capped by concrete, but a small opening − presumably for ventilation − covered by a grid, allows inspection.

Birchover, like Winster, is an ancient settlement and is recorded in the Domesday Book as 'Barcovere', meaning birch-covered steep slope. This probably refers to the hillside behind the buildings on the north side of the village. During the 19th and early part of this century gritstone quarrying for building stone supplied work for the village people. Most of the quarries, which lie northeast of Birchover on Stanton Moor, have become overgrown and some of them can be explored on the next walk (Route 2). If a visit to the Red Lion is included, a display of photographs of byegone quarrymen can be seen.

Before setting off back on the return leg of the walk, it is well worth the short diversion to Rowtor Rocks, which lie hidden by trees and bushes on the hillock behind the Druid Inn. The weird and mysterious features of this jumble of gritstone rocks have been associated with druidical practices! In addition to its strange natural features, there are some interesting man-made ones. The Reverend Thomas Eyre, who lived in the rectory below the rocks until his death in 1717, had seats carved in the rocks with a stone staircase for access. A word of caution for those with children, however; whilst exploring the rocks is fascinating, those on the north side are precipitous and extra vigilance is needed hereabouts.

The last 1½ miles back to Winster is not without interest, and there are good views southwards from several points along the way.

Refreshments

Birchover: Red Lion – bar lunches, coffee, tables and benches outside in summer. Druid Inn – meals and bar lunches, tea and coffee, tables on terrace. Winster: Miners Standard Inn – bar lunches, coffee. Bowling Green Inn – bar lunches, tea and coffee.

Access by bus

To both Winster and Birchover from Bakewell or Matlock (Hulleys and Countybus), Monday to Saturday.

Cottages in Birchover

13

Route 1

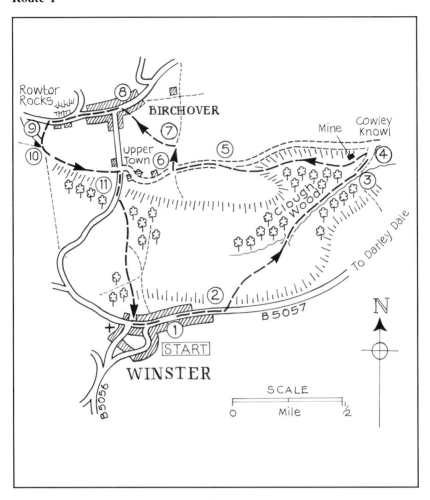

14

Route 1

Clough Wood and Rowtor Rocks 4½ miles

Start

At Winster, about 4 miles west of Matlock on the B5057. Park where it is not inconvenient for residents. No official car park (GR 242605).

Route

1. *Walk east out of Winster along the B5057 in the direction of Darley Dale. Continue beyond Winster Primary School for 200 metres to a stile on the left and opposite a gate on the right side of the road.*

2. *Cross the stile and bear right downhill along the obvious stiled footpath. Near the bottom of the hill the path virtually disappears in a field but the two pillars of a squeeze stile clearly mark the direction. Beyond the pillars, head for the left corner of the field to a stile. Cross this and a footbridge and continue along a woodland footpath. You are now in Clough Wood.*

3. *The path eventually emerges in a clearing with tracks and traces of past quarry workings. Keep on in the same general direction along a gradually ascending track. Follow it to where another track joins from the left immediately before a gate.*

4. *Turn sharp left along this track. Follow it past the ruins of the Cowley Knowl lead-mining engine house and shaft. Where the track ends, continue more or less straight ahead into the wood along a footpath. Follow this uphill to a stile at the top edge of the wood. Cross this and continue to another stile and a track.*

5. *Go left along the track. Follow it for about ¼ mile to a stile on the right which is on the left of a gate.*

6. *Cross the stile and continue along a field path for a short distance to the second stile on the left, which is a squeeze stile.*

7. *Go left here and continue, with a hedge on the left, to a gap in this hedge at the far end of the field. Go through the gap and turn right immediately to cross another stile which is hidden from view until you are almost upon it. Continue along the obvious stiled footpath to buildings and the road in Birchover.*

8. *Turn left and walk through the village (Red Lion on the right) to the sharp right-hand bend adjacent to the Druid Inn. Cross the road and follow the tarmac lane that runs alongside the inn. (Rowtor Rocks can be reached by steps on the right just after the inn). Continue along the lane to a wooden stile on the left.*

Continued on page 16

15

9. *Cross the stile and continue up to and across another stile to join another track. Turn left along the track. Keep straight on at a fork to a stile on the left of a gate.*

10. *Go through the stile, then turn left immediately to follow the path alongside the wall on the left. Continue along the obvious path to farm buildings and a narrow lane. This is Upper Town.*

11. *Turn right and walk down the steep lane to a stile on the left immediately after a right-hand bend. Cross this stile and continue along a field path that goes down into a dip, climbs again, then descends before the final uphill stretch into Winster. The path is paved in parts. Keep a more or less straight course, ignoring any other possibilities to left or right.*

Winster Market Hall

Stanton Moor

Outline

Rowsley − Stanton Woodhouse − Stanton Moor − Birchover − Stanton Moor − Congreave − Rowsley.

Summary

The longer walk and its variations all centre on Stanton Moor, a small but wild stretch of gritstone moorland with a Bronze Age cemetery and a famous stone circle. Well-used footpaths, tracks and two short sections on country lanes lead from Rowsley to Birchover and back. The walk passes through pastures, woodland and scrub as well as the more open heather-clad moorland sections on Stanton Moor, which is crossed twice en route to enable most of the interesting features to be viewed and explored. Although most of the hill-climbing is done in the first two miles, the longer walk described is only recommended for those used to regular walking outings.

Attractions

Often bypassed by tourists on their way to Bakewell, Matlock or Chatsworth, Rowsley is an attractive little settlement of stone cottages and has a water-powered flour mill which is open to tourists (see Route 3 for details). In the 19th century Rowsley attracted artists, poets and anglers, many of whom would have stayed at the Peacock Hotel, which was built in the 'Peak style' in 1652 as a gentlemen's residence. It was the coming of the Midland Railway in 1849, however, which brought prosperity to Rowsley. Up until this time, its trade in dressed building stone quarried from Stanton Moor had been fairly local. The coming of the railway meant a rapid expansion in the trade since Rowsley was now linked directly to the growing towns and cities of Lancashire. The railway also brought hordes of tourists on their way to visit Chatsworth. They would alight at Rowsley Station, then continue their journey by horse-drawn carriage.

Leaving Rowsley and its memories behind, the walk gradually wends its way uphill and passes through the delightful cluster of cottages and farm buildings at Stanton Woodhouse. On from here, field paths through pasture and woodland lead up to the lane that circumnavigates Stanton Moor. A short way along this, access to the moor proper is gained, and one quickly arrives at the circle of stones known as Nine Ladies. Unlike the stone circle at Arbor Low, a henge monument which seems to have been a meeting place for religious practices, the Nine Ladies was originally a burial mound, and all but the inner circle of stones has long since been eroded away or removed by later human communities in the area.

En route to Birchover across the moor, many excavated barrows or burial mounds can be explored. Apparently, there are over seventy of these, erected by the Beaker Folk at some time between 1800 and 1000 BC. *Continued on page 21*

Route 2

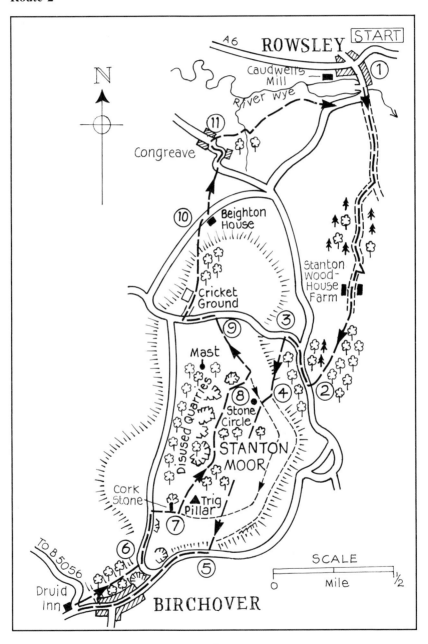

Route 2

Stanton Moor

7¼ miles (Shorter variations 6 miles and 3 miles)

Start

At Rowsley, 4 miles south of Bakewell on the A6. Park on the official parking spaces on the road signposted to Stanton-in-Peak and Caudwell's Mill (opposite the Peacock Hotel) (GR 257657).

Route

1. *Walk away from the main road along the minor road, passing a school, the entrance to Caudwell Mill's car park, and crossing a bridge. Keep straight on after the bridge along the lane to Stanton Woodhouse. This is a 'Private Road' but a public right of way. Ignore a left fork and continue uphill through woodland. The road surface degenerates into a rough track and zigzags right, then left above a house. Follow the track past farm buildings at Stanton Woodhouse, go straight on through a gate, then continue along the way-marked path. This soon bears right uphill to a ladder stile next to a gate. Cross this, then keep straight on as signposted for Stanton Lees ignoring a right fork, to reach a minor road via a stile.*

2. *Turn right along the road. Fork left after the chunky wall towards Stanton-in-Peak. Continue round a bend to a stepping stile on the left.*

3. *Cross this and keep straight on along the ascending path, ignoring other possibilities. Cross a wooden stile and take the right-hand footpath through the wood, staying on the left of a wall. Continue along a fence to a stile on the right.*

4. *Cross this and follow a path, forking left to the Nine Ladies stone circle. Just before the circle is reached a wide footpath is crossed. Return to this and, now with your back to the stone circle, turn right along it (southwest), ignoring all other possibilities. Continue across the moor to a crossroads of paths. Go straight on and down to a road via a stile.*

5. *Turn right along the road and follow it past an old quarry on the right. Fork left at a junction and walk down into Birchover. Continue through the village (Red Lion on the right) to the sharp right-hand bend adjacent to the Druid Inn. On the opposite side of the bend to the inn, take the footpath uphill. This climbs above the village and passes old quarry workings before reaching a minor road.*

6. *Turn left along the road and continue for ¼ mile to an obvious well-used footpath on the right with large boulders positioned to prevent parking. Follow this path across a stile and go as far as the Cork Stone, recognizable by its iron rungs placed to aid climbing.*

7. *Fork left at the Cork Stone to pass between old quarry workings on the left and a triangulation pillar on the right. Follow the footpath, staying fairly close to but on the right of further old quarry workings. The footpath eventually becomes vague and seems to end at a fence. Follow the fence to the right and stay with it until a large quarry is reached. Follow its perimeter fence to where it turns sharp left.*

8. *Leave the fence, and the quarry, here and go straight on for 50 metres to join a wide and well-used footpath. Turn left and follow this to a road.*

9. *Turn left along the road and walk to a footpath sign on the right at a track. Follow the track past a cricket ground, then straight on along a path through woods to a minor road.*

10. *Turn right along the road, then cross a stile on the left (Public Footpath sign) just past Beighton House. Go steeply down to a gateway, pass left of a derelict stone hut, and continue through a stile. Carry on to a gate and a lane. Turn left and go down the steep lane to a footpath sign on the right next to a cottage.*

11. *Turn right here, cross a stile and go straight on and down to a stream. **Immediately** after crossing the stream, turn right to cross a stile into the wood. In a few metres, you come out of the wood into a field via another stile. Once in the field, bear slightly right to a stile (no fence), then bear left along the more obvious grassy path to reach a road. Turn left along the road and follow it back to Rowsley.*

Shorter variations
3 miles *Start in Birchover, then follow the footpath above the village as for 5 above. Continue as for 6, 7 and 8 above as far as the wide well-used footpath. Turn right along this, continue to the stone circle, then as for 4 and 5 above to return to Birchover.* **6 miles** *As for 1 to 4 above as far as the crossroads of paths. Turn right here and continue to the Cork Stone. Turn right here to continue as for 7 to 11 above.*

Refreshments
Birchover: Druid Inn (meals and bar snacks, tea and coffee served, tables on terrace). Red Lion (bar snacks). Rowsley: Caudwell's Mill (pleasant cafe in interesting surroundings open most of the year).

Access by bus
To Rowsley from Derby and Manchester via Matlock, Bakewell, and Buxton daily (Trent). To Birchover from Bakewell and Matlock, Monday to Saturday (Hulleys).

For those on the longer walk, Birchover offers much-needed refreshments. The village also has some picturesque old stone cottages, the oddity of Rowtor Rocks (mentioned in Route 1), and a small factory at its eastern end producing high quality dressed stone for building. Originally a farming community, Birchover grew into the village it is today as a result of the quarrying industry for building stone, and the route back across Stanton Moor passes many of the former quarries. If a visit to the Red Lion is included, a small collection of photographs of quarrying in bygone days is displayed in the tap-room.

After climbing out of Birchover via the wooded ridge that gave the village its name, the openness of Stanton Moor is reached once more. One of the first features to be encountered is the Cork Stone, a 4 metre high block of gritstone with metal rungs cemented into it to enable the more agile and adventurous to climb to the top. However, 4 metres is a long way to jump or fall from, and youngsters need to be adequately supervised. This applies also for the following mile, which passes disused and overgrown quarries. These can be fun to explore but climbing should be dissuaded. In the more open stretches along the moor keep an eye out for skylarks and meadow pipits.

The descent from the moor offers fine views across the gritstone country to the north and the limestone plateau to the west. A combination of woodland paths and footpaths across open pastureland lead pleasantly back to Rowsley, where teas and home-made snacks can be enjoyed at Caudwell's Mill.

The Corkstone, Stanton Moor

Calton Lees

Outline

Calton Lees – Calton Houses – Rowsleymoor Wood – Rowsley – Beeley – Calton Lees.

Summary

Although the main walk and its shorter variation start at the same place and have a lot in common, they share only the first mile. From Calton Lees just outside Chatsworth Park, both walks trace a route up a quiet valley, make a short ascent of a hillside, pass through woodland, descend to a village and return to the starting point via pastures and riverside. The shorter walk calls in at Edensor and stays within the boundary of Chatsworth Park, whilst the longer walk includes a visit to the villages of Rowsley and Beeley. Well-defined paths and tracks are followed, and the walk through Rowsley includes a half a mile of roadside pavement. There are good views from the high points on both walks. *Although the short section between the Old Mill and the car park is not a public footpath, at the invitation of the Chatsworth Trustees, members of the public are welcome to walk in the park.*

Attractions

From the car park overlooking one of the most beautiful stretches of the River Derwent, the first interesting feature is the Saw Mill, where one can see the stockpiles of timber that have been cut from the Chatsworth plantations, much of which is destined for paper-mills, mining timber and fence posts. The wood is mainly Norway Spruce, Scots Pine and larch.

On from the saw mill the track begins to climb steadily, passing below Calton Lees Farm and the quaint little group of cottages next to it. Further up the valley, where there is woodland, it is not uncommon to see pheasant running to and fro across the track, since they seem to be partial to the undergrowth alongside the stream. Calton Houses is a small group of charming cottages in an idyllic situation with lovely views down the valley to the River Derwent and Beeley Moor beyond.

Whichever route is taken from Calton Houses, a short hill climb through pasture leads up to the top of a ridge, and coniferous woods are entered. Although these are man-made, they are not sterile areas of the countryside. Whilst passing through this particular woodland, you may see goldcrest, coal-tit and, occasionally, crossbill.

On the shorter walk, there are fine views across to Chatsworth House and Stand Wood as you descend to Edensor, the estate village. This was newly constructed in the 1830s following the demolition of the original village. Apparently, the old village was in full view of Chatsworth House, which the Duke found offensive, so he ordered its removal to its present position. Joseph Paxton, who designed many of the features in Chatsworth Park, played a large part in designing the houses and their layout at the new Edensor. His grave can be seen in the churchyard, which is passed en route. The village has a splendid tea-shop, which is also the Post Office, and it is well worth sampling their cream teas.

Pleasant walking through the parkland follows and leads down to the bridge a little distance beyond which is Queen Mary's Bower. This is an interesting structure that may well have been used by Mary Queen of Scots during her incarceration at Chatsworth in the 1570s. A riverside stroll continues the journey as far as the ruined flour mill, built around 1760 and operating until 1950. Unfortunately, a tree fell on the building in a gale in 1962 and the mill was left to ruin.

On the longer walk, there are fine views across the Wye valley, before the descent is made through Manner's Wood. In contrast to the coniferous plantations on top of the ridge, Manner's Wood is natural woodland with a considerable variety of trees and shrubs. Amongst the bird species that inhabit these woods, the tree-creeper is fairly common, and a little patience should reward you with a sighting of one of these unusual birds.

On emerging from the woods, a further descent leads to Rowsley with its special attraction of Caudwell's Mill, a working water-powered flour mill open to visitors. Built in 1874, the mill is a unique example of a working turbine-driven water mill. As well as this, there is glass-blowing and various other craft workshops and a welcoming cafe on the site.

On the way back from Rowsley, the walk drops in at Beeley with its attractive 17th century cottages, a 17th century inn and a gem of a church that dates from the 13th century.

Refreshments

At Edensor: tea-shop. At Calton Lees car park: teas and snacks kiosk. At Rowsley: Caudwell's Mill cafe. At Beeley: Devonshire Arms, bar lunches and meals, tea and coffee available. Family room, tables and benches at front of pub.

Access by bus

To Chatsworth from Matlock and Buxton (East Midland), Sundays and Bank Holiday Mondays.

Route 3

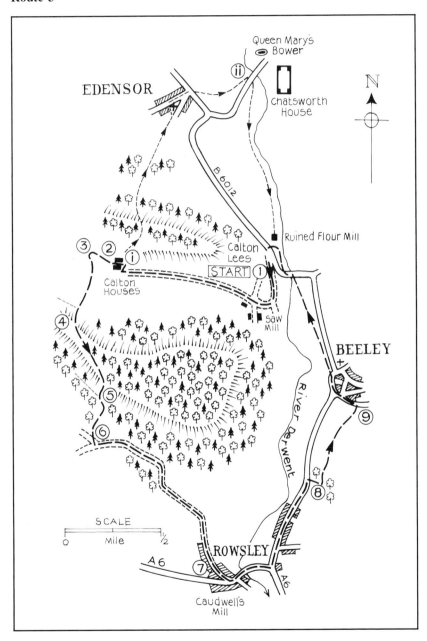

Route 3

Calton Lees

5½ miles (Shorter variation 4 miles)

Start

At Calton Lees car park, Chatsworth Park, just off the B6012 a mile north of Beeley and a mile south of Edensor (GR 258685).

Route

1. *From the car park, walk south along the lane towards the Garden Centre. Stay on this lane (signposted Forest Office and Saw Mill) and follow it past the Saw Mill and round to the right. Keep straight on up the valley for about one mile to Calton Houses. Continue past the cottages and keep straight on along a walled path to a gate.*

2. *Go through the gate, turn left and follow the wall on the left alongside the wood. This leads to a gate and stile on the left at the end of the first wood.*

3. *Cross this stile, then bear left with the footpath. In a short distance, the path bends up to the right to the woods at the top of the hillside.*

4. *Continue across a stile, then straight on along a well-used and blue-waymarked path through the woodland. This bends left and descends through more woodland, then reaches another footpath.*

5. *Turn left along this, and in 50 metres fork right downhill along another path. Continue down to a crossroads of tracks.*

6. *Turn left (yellow waymark). Stay on this track-cum-footpath as it winds its way gradually down into Rowsley village and to the A6. (Caudwell's Mill is across the road a little to the right.)*

7. *Go left on the pavement alongside the A6, over the bridge and to the junction with the B6012, signposted to Sheffield, Chatsworth and Baslow. Follow the B6012 past houses for about ½ mile from the junction to a garage on the left. Continue for a further 100 metres or so to a stile and footpath on the right signposted to Beeley.*

8. *Cross this stile, follow the path through a wood on the left of a stream to a stile on the left. Cross this, then keep straight on alongside the wall on the left. Apart from a small diversion when you walk with the wall/fence on your right, you keep the wall/fence on your left. This leads to a minor road.*

9. *Turn left along the road and into Beeley. Turn right at the main road and walk*

along the pavement to the start of a footpath on the left, opposite a road on the right. Follow the path across riverside meadows to the old bridge leading into Chatsworth Park. Cross the bridge, then go right at a kissing gate and walk to the ruined flour mill. Walk up to the left to the car park.

Shorter variation

Although this walk shares the first mile with the longer route, it is essentially a different walk, taking in the area to the north of Calton Lees.

As for 1 above to the gate, then: (i) go through the gate and turn right. Follow the path uphill and into the woodland on the ridge. Follow the bridleway through the woodland, then head straight down the hillside into Edensor entering the village at a small gate to the left of the church. Descend the steps straight ahead and then turn right. (The tea-shop is on the right just past the church). Continue to and across the B6012 and follow the gravel path opposite up through trees then down to the bridge. ii Turn right and follow the river for a mile to the old flour mill. Turn right to go up to the car park.

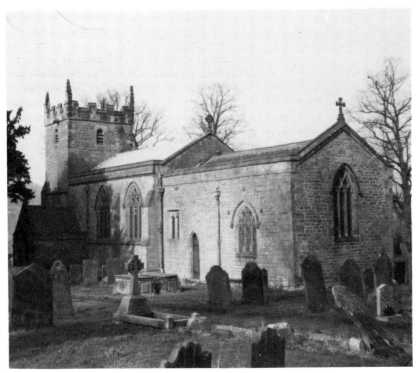

Beeley Church

26

Haddon Fields and Lathkill Dale

Outline
Bakewell − Haddon Hall − Conksbury Bridge − Over Haddon − Bakewell.

Summary
Starting from Bakewell, the route follows the meandering River Wye as far as Haddon Hall. From here, a gradual ascent leads up on to the limestone plateau to the west of the Wye valley. A short, sharp descent into Lathkill Dale follows, and a pleasant and fairly easy amble alongside the River Lathkill with its lovely weirs and crystal clear water leads to Lathkill Lodge. A short but steep climb follows into Over Haddon, perched above and overlooking the dale. Leaving Over Haddon, a descent via footpaths and a little section of country lane is made into Bakewell.

Attractions
Bakewell holds enough interest to warrant several visits. Its origins date from the Iron Age or earlier, although its name is of Saxon origin, meaning Beadeca's spring. By the 13th century Bakewell was already an important market town, and in the 18th century Richard Arkwright built a water-powered textile mill here. As well as its historic buildings and relics (some of which are mentioned in Route 5), and the fact that it acts as a centre for tourists to the Peak District, one of its special points of interest is the weekly Monday market which attracts folk from all over the region. The stalls are adjacent to the livestock market and the whole atmosphere reflects the extent to which Bakewell is a focal point, a meeting place, for the inhabitants of the villages and farms of the Peak District.

From Bakewell, the walk begins as an easy stroll down the valley shaped by the River Wye. Along this section, mallard, coot, moorhen and the less conspicuous dipper might be seen. The riverside walk continues as far as the boundary of Haddon Hall, whose battlemented, mediaeval architecture can be viewed from the footpath. The oldest parts of the building date from 1080-90 and various development continued until the 16th century, since when little has been altered.

From Haddon Hall, the route climbs out of the valley westwards through Haddon Fields up on to the limestone plateau, and from here there are extensive views across the central Peak District. This is also curlew country, although you are more likely to hear rather than spot them.

Just before descending into Lathkill Dale, the footpath passes the spoil heaps of Raper Mine, where fluorspar was extracted for use in the making of steel. Beyond the mine a short descent leads down to the River Lathkill, which is crossed by an old and narrow packhorse bridge. And on the opposite side of the river is Raper Lodge, a fine looking residence which appeared in the film 'The Virgin and the Gypsy', based

Continued on page 31

27

Route 4

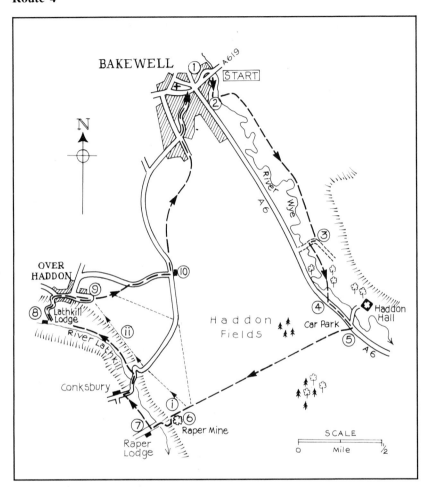

Route 4

Haddon Fields and Lathkill Dale 5¾ miles (Shorter variation 5 miles)

Start

At Bakewell. Park in one of the public pay and display car parks. The walk is described from the centre of Bakewell (GR 218685).

Route

1. From the town centre walk northeast out towards the river along the A619. Immediately before crossing the river, branch right to gain the riverside footpath. Follow this downstream to a footbridge.

2. Go over the footbridge and keep straight on to cross a second footbridge, then turn right. Continue past playing fields and keep straight on along the footpath that follows the river's direction (not its meanders) downstream.

3. After a mile, turn right along a lane, then turn left along the continuation of the riverside footpath. In about ⅓ mile, the A6 is reached alongside the grounds of Haddon Hall after crossing over the Wye.

4. Turn left along the pavement and walk as far as the entrance to Haddon Hall.

5. Cross the main road (with care) to the footpath signposted to Youlgreave. Follow this in a straight line uphill, first with the wall on the right, then with the wall on the left. Stiles mark the way. In a little over a mile, with farm buildings on the left, a stile is reached in the wall ahead. (After wet weather, and if the last 200 metres look badly churned by cattle, make a wide sweep to the right, then follow the wall back to the stile.)

6. Cross the stile and continue straight on to a wooden stile in the fence on the left or a little further to a handgate. Whichever route is taken, bear left downhill at the far end of old mine workings/spoil heaps. The path becomes a narrow track that winds very steeply down to the River Lathkill. Cross an old packhorse bridge to a stile and signpost for Lathkill Dale on the right, before Raper Lodge.

7. Cross the stile and walk upstream to a minor road. Turn right along this (Conksbury Farm refreshments to the left), cross Conksbury Bridge, then turn left to regain the riverside footpath, now on the right bank. Follow it to Lathkill Lodge, where there is also a footbridge and a ford.

8. Turn right and walk up the steep lane. Turn right at the first road on the right and continue to the Lathkill Hotel.

29

9. *From the hotel continue through the stile adjacent to it, go past the tree stump and keep straight on (ignoring the right fork leading downhill) to and across a double stile. Fork left and continue via stiles to a road. Turn right and continue to a T-junction.*

10. *Turn left and walk for 150 metres to a stile and signpost on the right. Cross the stile (narrow!), then take the left fork. Follow the clearly defined footpath, crossing stiles and dipping down and out of a shallow valley. Continue along a walled path, past a school to a road, then keep straight on past houses to a junction. Fork right down a pedestrian way and into the centre of Bakewell.*

Shorter variation

As for 1 to 5 above, then:

i. *Cross the stile as for 6 above and fork right instead of carrying on in the same direction. continue to a minor road via stiles. Cross the road and continue in the same direction to a stile. Cross it and follow the path with views of Lathkill Dale below.*

ii *Bear right with the main footpath up through a field to the stile adjacent to the Lathkill Hotel. Continue as for 9 and 10 above.*

Haddon Hall seen from Haddon Fields

on the novel by D.H. Lawrence. The riverside footpath leads to another old and sturdily built packhorse bridge at Conksbury. This carries the road that links Bakewell with Youlgreave. The farmhouse at Conksbury sells teas and refreshments in the summer months which can be enjoyed in the farm garden.

Upstream from here, the dale becomes a gorge with steep, wooded slopes, and the river falls over a succession of weirs which create a remarkable sight. Throughout this section, flitting about near the river bank, you might see both grey and the less common yellow wagtail. Both birds have yellow underparts but the grey wagtail is blue-grey above whilst the yellow wagtail is greenish-brown.

The riverside walk goes as far as Lathkill Lodge, next to it is Sour Mill, a former water-powered cornmill dating from about 1529 and worked until the early 19th century. Leaving the dale at this point, a steep, albeit short, ascent leads into Over Haddon, a little hamlet which is, literally, perched above the valley of the River Lathkill. And because of its position above the dale, there are fine views across to Youlgreave and Harthill Moor beyond. As luck − or perhaps design − would have it, the Lathkill Hotel and its south facing terrace is undoubtedly the best viewpoint in the hamlet. Whilst the grown-ups are taking in the scenery and relaxing with refreshments purchased from the hostelry, youngsters can play in the field adjacent or climb and explore the hollow tree stump. What is more, the remainder of the walk is on the level or downhill back into Bakewell.

Refreshments
At Over Haddon − Lathkill Hotel, pub food, tea and coffee, ample safe space for outside drinking, fine views. At Bakewell − Original Bakewell Pudding Shop − Country Kitchen − several more cosy tea-shops and a snack bar − Red Lion: meals and bar lunches, coffee, chairs and tables in rear yard in summer season − Tavern Bar (Rutland Arms Hotel): meals and bar lunches, tea and coffee, table and chairs in courtyard, children admitted. Open all day during the summer.

Access by bus
Bakewell is well-served by bus from Sheffield (PMT, SYT), from Manchester and Buxton (Trent) and from Derby and Matlock (Trent).

Manner's Wood and Wye Valley

Outline
Bakewell − Manner's Wood − Haddon Park − Bakewell.

Summary
This is a delightful walk, sheltered and ideal for a cold and windy day. The first part climbs quite steeply out of Bakewell, then traverses the length of Manner's Wood high above the River Wye, which is glimpsed from time to time where the trees thin out. The return leg of the walk is a pleasant ramble through riverside meadows alongside the slow-moving and meandering Wye. On a dry day, when footwear was kept unmuddied, a visit to Haddon Hall could be incorporated, adding a mile to the route (NB Haddon Hall is closed on Sundays for most of the year.)

Attractions
Bakewell is known as the 'Gateway to the Peak'. Being the only sizeable town within the boundary of the Peak District National Park, it plays a central role for tourists. As well as its shops, cafes and pubs, there are many buildings of historical interest. It was a settlement in prehistoric times, however, and an Iron Age fort overlooks Bakewell from Ball Cross, ½ mile northeast of the town. This is thought to have been a Brigantian stronghold.

In Bakewell churchyard there is a large collection of carved stones from Saxon and Norman times as well as a splendid eight-foot high Saxon cross-shaft with decorative panels. The church itself is of Saxon origin, although the present building is mainly 19th century. Above the church is the Old House Museum, built as a parsonage in 1534 and now exhibiting artefacts of early domestic life in the region. The town has a 17th-century market hall which now houses an information and exhibition centre on the Peak District. The bridge over the Wye that connects the two parts of Bakewell dates from the 14th century, and its five Gothic arches seem to be able to cope admirably with the volume of modern traffic that passes over it.

The woodland part of the walk is pure delight. The trees that clothe this west-facing slope are a mixture of deciduous and coniferous varieties, and because they are not so densely packed as in many of the plantations, sunlight gets through the forest canopy, providing the right conditions for many species of wildflower and shrub to thrive. You may come across red campion, bluebell, wood sorrel, dog's mercury and dog rose amongst others. As to the birdlife, this is equally varied and the habitat of many woodland species, including the jay, wood pigeon, coal-tit, tree-creeper and both green and spotted woodpeckers.

After descending once more to the valley, a relatively short diversion downstream brings Haddon Hall into view. A medieval manor house with a history that dates back to the Norman conquest, it has been described as "the finest medieval country house in England", and a visit should be on everybody's itinerary at some time or other.

On the way back along the riverside, you may well catch sight of a dipper. About the size of a blackbird, its distinguishing feature is its white chest resembling a bib. It is most often seen standing on a rock in the river, bobbing and dipping, hence its name. Although the dipper can swim both on and under the surface, this remarkable bird also walks under water on the stream bed.

Refreshments

None en route. At Bakewell — Original Bakewell Pudding Shop — Country Kitchen — several more tea-shops and a snack bar — Red Lion: meals and bar lunches, coffee, chairs and tables in rear yard in summer season — Tavern Bar (Rutland Arms Hotel): meals and bar lunches, tea and coffee, table and chairs in courtyard, children admitted. Open all day during the summer.

Access by bus

Bakewell is well served by bus from Sheffield (PMT, SYT), from Manchester and Buxton (Trent) and from Derby and Matlock (Trent).

River Wye at Bakewell

33

Route 5

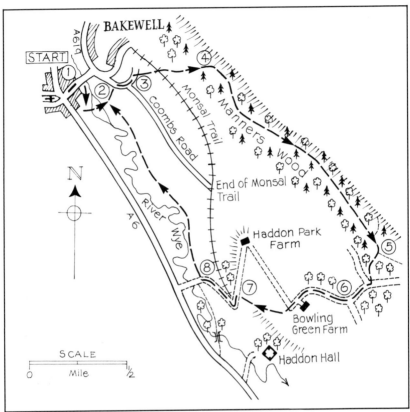

Treecreeper. Brown above, silvery-white below. Curved brown bill

Route 5

Manner's Wood and Wye Valley 4½ miles

Start

At Bakewell. Park in one of the public pay and display car parks. The walk is described from the centre of Bakewell (GR 218685).

Route

1. Walk along the A619 towards the river. Immediately before crossing the river, branch right to gain the riverside footpath. Follow this downstream to a footbridge. This is signposted to Coombs Road, your first objective. Cross this and a second footbridge, at the far end of which is a gate. Go through the gate, then bear left through a handgate. Continue through a car park to Coombs Road.

2. Turn right along the road and continue past houses to a track on the left signposted to Outrake Farm and Cottages.

3. Follow this track, go through the gate that leads to Outrake Farm, then continue straight on alongside a wall on the right where the farm track bends to the left. Continue across the Monsal Trail (a disused railway track) to reach a stile by a gate, then follow the footpath through the golf course. On leaving the golf course the footpath winds up into Manner's Wood. Follow this to where it forks.

4. Take the right fork. This soon joins another footpath at a T-junction of paths. Turn right here and follow the footpath and bridleway, which climbs steadily for about ½ mile then levels out. About ½ mile further on, another footpath joins from the left. Continue straight on for a few metres past this point to a fork in the path.

5. Take the right fork, which goes downhill and bends to the left before reaching a crossroads of tracks. Go straight across and continue along this farm track, rising gradually until a fork is reached.

6. Take the right fork and follow this track alongside a wood, then down past Bowling Green Farm. Continue past the farm entrance to where the track bends sharply right at a gate. Leave the track here and carry on in the same direction along the waymarked footpath/bridlepath. In a short distance, this turns right at an iron fence, which is followed to where it ends at a stile at a tarmaced lane.

7. Turn left along the lane. Follow it over a disused railway, at which point the lane doubles back downhill to the River Wye and the A6. Continue along the lane to a handgate on the right before the bridge. (If a visit to Haddon Hall is to be included, follow the riverside footpath downstream, then turn left on the A6. Retrace your steps.)

8. *Turn right here and go through the handgate, then follow the way-marked route along the river valley. At the second river bend encountered, bear slightly left, ignoring a gateway that leads into a field. Continue past a rugby ground to reach the second of the two footbridges crossed at the start of the walk. Retrace your steps to the car park or bus stop.*

Old market cross, Gt. Longstone

Ashford, Monsal Trail and Monsal Head

Outline

Ashford — Churchdale Farm — Monsal Trail — Little Longstone —
Monsal Head — Ashford.

Summary

The walk follows footpaths and the Monsal Trail, a disused railway track, in the
limestone countryside north of Ashford-in-the-Water. A gradual ascent to Little
Longstone — with the option to visit Great Longstone as well — and Monsal Head
is rewarded with one of the most spectacular views in the Peak District. The walk
continues to climb for a short distance beyond Monsal Head towards the summit of
Fin Cop, once the site of an Iron Age fort. From the high point on the walk there are
panoramic views of the limestone countryside. A sharp descent leads back down to
Ashford.

Attractions

Ashford-in-the-Water is a particularly picturesque village situated at a widening in the
valley of the River Wye. Although its name is of Saxon derivation — meaning 'ford
of the ash' — tools and weapons made from the flint-like chert found amongst the scree
slopes nearby are a clear indication that nomadic Stone Age hunters often passed this
way as they followed the migrating reindeer. Ashford's present church was rebuilt in
1869 but the original one was Norman. In the 17th century the beautiful Sheepwash
Bridge was built to carry packhorse trains taking malt from Derby across the River
Wye. The village used to have several mills but only one, said to be ancient, still
survives. This is Flewitt's Mill, situated at the lower end of Ashford. A corn mill,
it used to have two water wheels but now corn is ground by water-powered turbine.

After climbing out of the valley, the walk joins the Monsal Trail, the disused
railway track of the former Midland Railway. Linking Buxton with Bakewell, it was
not only a major feat of 19th-century engineering but one of the most scenically
spectacular lines in the country. Since the closure of the line in 1968, the disused
tracks, the cuttings and embankments, have become the habitat for many species of
wildflower, some of which are rare for the region. Amongst these you may see the
Nottingham catchfly, kidney vetch and bloody cranesbill. Great Longstone station is
passed along this section of the Monsal Trail, the station building is now a private
residence.

If the variation taking in Great Longstone is followed, it is well worth the short
diversion to see the 14th century church. Great Longstone is a typical limestone village
whose wealth was founded on lead mining and livestock farming. Inside the church
two old carvings depict these two forms of industry, one being a lead miner, the other
a milkmaid.

Continued on page 41

37

Route 6

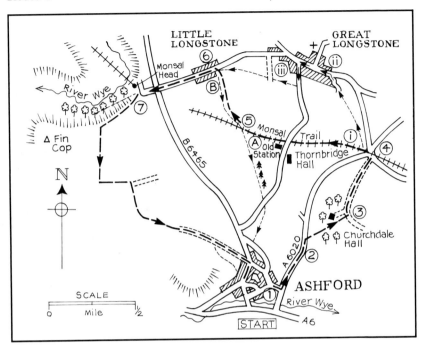

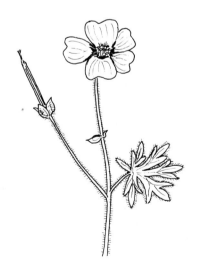

Bloody Cranesbill. June – August (Purple-red)

38

Route 6

Ashford, Monsal Trail and Monsal Head
5 miles (Variations of 5, 4 and 3 miles)

Start

At Ashford-in-the-Water, 2 miles west of Bakewell just off the A6. Park in the official car park situated near the back (north side) of the church (GR 195697).

Route

1. *Return to the main street through the village and walk to the junction with the A6020. Turn left and walk on the pavement alongside the A6020 for about ¼ mile, looking carefully for a stile with carved posts in the hedge on the right hand side of the road.*

2. *Cross the road and go through this stile, then a handgate, and follow the path as it bears left and up an embankment. Follow the footpath across a stile, a field and another stile, then bear left alongside a wall. With the wall on your left, continue to a track.*

3. *Turn left along the track to join a tarmac drive (Churchdale Hall is on the left.) Turn right along the drive and follow it to a road (A6020). Cross the road, go under the railway bridge and turn right immediately to gain access to the Monsal Trail, the disused railway track that crosses the bridge.*

4. *Turn right along the trail, cross the bridge and continue for about ¾ mile − passing Great Longstone Station − to a sign that says 'No Through Way Ahead'.*

5. *Turn right, cross the stile and follow the waymarked path to the road at Little Longstone.*

6. *Turn left along the road and continue through the village and on to the road junction at Monsal Head (there is a pavement along the whole of this stretch). Cross the road, walk past the front of the Monsal Head Hotel and the cafe and go through the stile.*

7. *Take the **second** narrow footpath on the left as signposted for Ashford. This goes up to a wall, then continues with the wall on the left and the dale on the right. A gradual ascent is made towards the summit of Fin Cop until a stepping stile is reached. Cross the stile and continue, now away from the dale, along the obvious path. Soon, the path turns sharp left over a stile and, in a short distance, turns sharp right at another stile. Keep straight on along this path, which becomes a track that leads back into Ashford-in-the-Water. Turn right to finish.*

Variations

A 5 mile variation taking in Great Longstone

As for 1 to 3 above as far as the railway bridge.

i. *After passing under the bridge, turn left immediately, cross a stile with a signpost to Great Longstone, and walk along the narrow footpath to a stile on the right (to continue along this path would bring you up on to the Monsal Trail). Cross the stile and follow the well-used field path into Great Longstone.*

ii. *Turn left along the road that passes through the village and continue to Station Road on the left.*

iii. *Go left along Station Road and continue for about 150 metres to a stile on the right. Cross this and continue straight on for ½ mile, crossing a track on the way, along the stile footpath to Little Longstone. Continue as for 6 and 7 above.*

Shorter variations

A. **3 miles.** *As for 1 to 4 above, then cross the stile on the left-hand side. Follow this path down for ½ mile to and across a lane, then continue for ¼ mile to and across the wider B6465 to a minor road. Turn left to finish.*

B. **4 miles.** *As for the 5-mile variation to the road at Little Longstone, then turn left immediately to follow the footpath leading to the Monsal Trail. On reaching the trail, cross it via the stiles and continue as for the 3 mile walk back to Ashford.*

Monsal Trail, Gt. Longstone station

40

Monsal Head

A little further on is Little Longstone, a roadside hamlet that also has a long history of lead mining and farming. Its quaint cottages date mainly from the 17th and 18th centuries, and the Packhorse Inn has a very welcoming appearance as well as a beer garden.

Not far from this quiet little spot is Monsal Head, with its hotel, tea-shops and ice cream van. From this point, there is one of the most spectacular views in the Peak District, for Monsal Head is situated above the deep gorge of Monsal Dale, its proportions enhanced by the presence of the Monsal Viaduct heading straight into the valley side.

The way back passes above the dale and its tree-clad slopes, the view constantly changing. A footpath leads tantalisingly close to the summit of Fin Cop, the Iron Age fort, but alas there is no public right of way and the path suddenly plunges southwards along its eastern flank. As with the Iron Age fort on Mam Tor, only earthen ramparts and ditches remain. On the way down to Ashford, there are particularly fine views both east and south across the limestone plateau.

Refreshments
At Ashford — Bull's Head: pub food, tea and coffee, wooden tables in front of pub, children admitted — Ashford Hotel: meals and bar lunches, tea and coffee, beer garden — tea-shop and tea-garden. At Great Longstone — White Lion: meals and bar food, tea and coffee, beer garden and tables in front of pub. At Little Longstone — Packhorse Inn: bar food, tea and coffee, beer garden. At Monsal Head — Monsal Head Hotel: bar meals and bar snacks, tea and coffee, beer garden, marquee in inclement weather, tea-room — tea-shops.

Access by bus
To Ashford from Stockport, Buxton, Bakewell and Matlock (Trent) every day. Also from Castleton and Bakewell (Hulley's), Monday to Saturday only.

Baslow Edge

Outline
Baslow Edge − Wellington's Monument − Curbar Gap − Curbar − Calver − Baslow.

Summary
Starting at Nether End, the east side of Baslow, a track is soon joined that climbs steeply uphill for a mile and gains the top of Baslow Edge at Wellington's Monument. From here, the rest is on the level or downhill. A footpath is followed along the top of Baslow Edge to the break at Curbar Gap. Along this section, there are splendid views west to Longstone Moor and the limestone plateau and south to Chatsworth Park and beyond. From Curbar Gap, a combination of footpaths and country lanes lead down through the village of Curbar to Calver and the River Derwent. The last leg of the walk is an easy stroll, at first alongside the river, then along the quiet lane that leads via the hamlet of Bubnell back into Baslow. On a windy day this walk is exposed to the elements and appropriate clothing is essential.

Attractions
The steep climb out of Baslow is rewarded by fine views from Wellington's Monument, although youngsters will probably get more enjoyment from scrambling on the rocks below the monument. This was erected in 1866 by an E.M. Wrench of the 34th Regiment to commemorate the Duke. In a south-easterly direction across the valley and clearly visible above Birchen Edge is Nelson's Monument, erected in 1810 by John Brightman of Baslow.

A stone's throw from Wellington's Monument is the Eaglestone. This is a prominent block of gritstone that has obviously offered more resistance to weathering and erosion than the rock that once surrounded it. Many years ago, it was a custom for the young men of Baslow to climb the Eaglestone to show their fitness for the responsibilities of marriage − no mean feat, since there are no easy ways up or down off this huge block!

Across the moorland section to Curbar Gap, there is a choice of footpaths. One heads more or less straight across the moor but a more interesting route is along the top of Baslow Edge − unless it is windy!

The 'edges' of Stanage, Froggatt, Curbar and Baslow are formed of a sandstone known as Millstone Grit. Millions of years ago, when this part of the British Isles was under the sea, gritty sands eroded from the rocks of mountains to the north were washed down by big rivers and deposited as layers on the sea bed on top of the newly formed limestone. These layers were compressed and solidified to form the gritstones of the Pennines. In turn, weathering of the gritstone reduces it to sand once again.

It is also interesting to compare the vegetation as you walk along the Edge. On the moor top, this is dominated by heather and moor grasses. Below the Edge bilberry, bracken and rowan have colonised the slopes. Further down are the pastures of cultivated lowland grasses and down by the river trees thrive.

The way down from Curbar Gap passes through the village of Curbar. At a crossroads in the middle of the village the decorative stone surrounds marking the spring that supplied fresh water for the inhabitants before mains water was laid on is worth investigating. Continuing downhill you arrive at Calver at the bottom of the hill, which has a welcoming inn and a craft centre and cafe. Also of interest is Calver Mill. Built in 1786, it now produces stainless steel sinks but was originally a water-powered spinning mill. Being quite a large mill, it would have provided work for many of the village folk.

Leaving Calver, a riverside footpath is followed, from where coot, moorhen and mallard are commonly sighted. The path also passes through a small slice of sycamore woodland where wild garlic and butterbur try to impede progress in summer. The last part of the walk gives you the opportunity to explore Bubnell and Baslow, both of which have interesting old buildings. Linking Bubnell and Baslow is a fine old bridge built in 1603 to replace an earlier wooden one. It is apparently the only bridge across the Derwent never to have been destroyed. And on the east side of the bridge there is the Watchman's Hut, a stone shelter just large enough to accommodate one person.

Refreshments
At Calver — Bridge Inn: bar lunches, coffee. — Derbyshire Craft Centre and Cafe. At Baslow — Tea-shop — Wheatsheaf Hotel: meals and bar lunches, tea and coffee, beer garden, children's play area adjacent to beer garden, also barbeques in summer, weather permitting.

Access by bus
Baslow is well-served by bus from Sheffield, Leek and Buxton (PMT), from Chesterfield and Buxton (East Midland), from Sheffield and Bakewell (SYT), and from Manchester and Chesterfield (Hulley's).

Wood-Warbler.
Greenish-brown above, with yellow breast and white underparts. Yellow eyestripe

43

Route 7

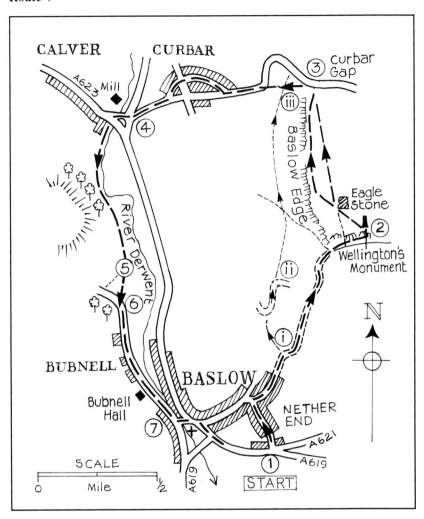

Route 7

Baslow Edge

5 miles (Shorter variation
4½ miles)

Start

At Baslow, Nether End. This part of the village lies between the bridge that carries the A619 over the River Derwent and the roundabout at the junction of the A621 with the A619. Park in the pay and display car park (GR 257722).

Route

1. With your back to the car park, cross the main road and go up the street on the immediate right of Crofter's Cafe (Eaton Hill). Continue to the junction with School Lane, then turn right and follow the lane uphill. This soon degenerates into a track. Continue for about ¾ mile to a handgate. Go through this. The footpath from here soon leads to the top of the moor and Wellington's Monument.

2. Turn left at Wellington's Monument and walk along a path of sorts to the prominent rock, the Eaglestone. From here, either follow the obvious wide path along the moor top or, more interesting, bear left across heather from the Eaglestone to Baslow Edge, then bear right along the minor footpath along the top of the edge. Both paths lead to the road at Curbar Gap.

3. Turn left at the road and walk downhill for about 150 metres to a stile on the left (Public Footpath sign). Cross this stile and continue downhill, passing a crossroads of footpaths. Go through a keyhole stile and continue straight down to rejoin the road further downhill. From here: **either** follow the road all the way down to a junction opposite the Bridge Inn; **or**, better, turn right after 300 metres at The Green, follow it round and across a minor junction in Curbar, then along Pinfold Hill to rejoin the road from Curbar Gap, where you turn right for the Bridge Inn.

4. Turn right to cross the bridge, then immediately left along a tarmac footpath. Continue behind houses, then along the riverside footpath.

5. After about ¾ mile, at a fork in the path, take the left branch to a lane via a keyhole stile.

6. Turn left at the lane and continue into Bubnell as far as the first river bridge on the left.

7. Cross this into Baslow, then turn right and walk along the pavement, passing the traffic island en route, back to the start.

Shorter variation

Start as for the longer walk and follow the track uphill but only as far as the first sharp right-hand bend with a gate and stile on the left, then:

i. *Cross the stile and follow the gradually ascending footpath, crossing two further stiles, to reach a bend in a track.*

ii. *Go right along the track and through a gateway. At this point, instead of following the track uphill to the right, keep straight on alongside the wall on the left. Continue to a footpath crossroads, keep straight on here then pass through a handgate further on. Carry on to another footpath crossroads. (If you reach a stile at a road, you have overshot the footpath crossroads.)*

iii. *Turn left to pass through a keyhole stile and continue straight down to join the road from Curbar Gap. Follow one of the options described in 3 above then continue as for 4 to 7 above.*

The watchman's hut on the old bridge at Baslow

46

Three Edges from Curbar Gap

Outline
Curbar Gap – White Edge – Grouse Inn – Froggatt Edge – Curbar Edge – Curbar Gap.

Summary
For its length, this is a relatively easy walk which, apart from the initial climb to White Edge and the descent to the Grouse Inn, is on the level. However, since there is little in the way of shelter and the walk is very exposed to the elements, a calm, dry day is recommended. There is plenty of space on this route and it is particularly suitable for those who enjoy wilderness. There are also extensive views over the Derwent valley and across to the limestone moors of the central Peak District. Well-defined paths are followed throughout.

Attractions
Soon after leaving the car park at Curbar Gap, you enter an area of moorland of the Eastern Moors Estate designated as a Wildlife Sanctuary. Although at first glance the 'wildlife' might appear to be rather limited, a closer examination of the surroundings reveals variety in the vegetation which, in turn, supports a wide number of species of insects, birds and small mammals. On the moorland slopes the most common grass species are tussocky mat grass and sheep's fescue. Other plants on the slopes include heath bedstraw, crowberry and bilberry. In the most unsheltered and exposed places heather tends to be the dominant species because, with its small leaves and slow growth, it is well adapted to the harsher weather conditions.

The walk along the top of the escarpment of White Edge passes through an area colonised by rabbits, and you would be unlucky not to see at least one at fairly close range. In the summer, the wheatear can be seen flitting from one rock perch to another. In flight, it can be distinguished from other small birds by its white rump. You are also likely to see meadow pipits and skylarks hereabouts.

White Edge is wilder and more open than Froggatt and Curbar Edges, and for this reason there is ample opportunity for youngsters to explore and scramble on the rocks below the path. And anywhere along White Edge would be ideal for a picnic stop.

After descending to the Grouse Inn, the footpath above Froggatt Edge is followed. Little diversions into the birch woodland along paths leading to viewpoints provide interest. When these are left behind, a small stone circle on the left of the path can be investigated. Early antiquaries called such stone circles druidic but we now know that they were built many centuries before the Druids were first mentioned in history. This stone circle, like the Nine Ladies stone circle on Stanton Moor and several more in the Peak District, was constructed by the Beaker Folk, people of the Bronze Age.

Continued on page 50

Route 8

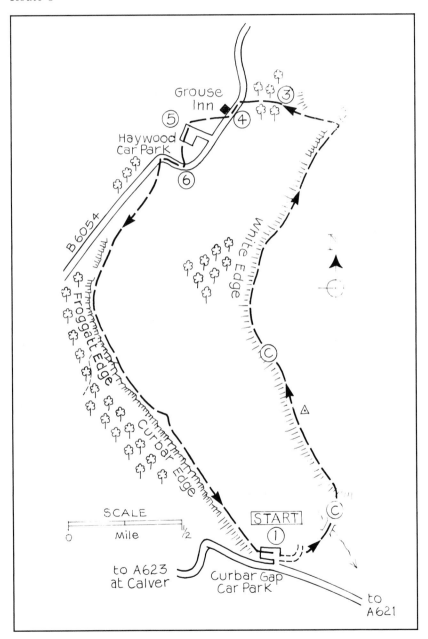

Grouse Inn

⑤ Haywood Car Park

④ ③

⑥

B 6054

White Edge

Froggatt Edge

Curbar Edge

Ⓒ

△

Ⓒ

SCALE

0   Mile   ½

START
①

to A623 at Calver

Curbar Gap Car Park

to A621

Route 8

Three Edges from Curbar Gap 5½ miles

Start

At Curbar Gap car park, situated between the A623 and A621 about ¾ mile east of Calver, which lies 2 miles north of Baslow (GR 262747). The walk could also be started at Haywood car park, situated on the B6054 just south of the Grouse Inn (GR 256777).

Route

1. *Facing the car park from the entrance, cross a stile on the right which is on the left of a gate and handgate. Continue along a track. Where it bears left, keep straight on into the Wildlife Sanctuary, as waymarked. Follow this footpath down and across a footbridge then uphill. Follow the signposted footpath for Longshaw along the top of the escarpment. Continue for about 2 miles, following White Edge to prominent rocks just before a wall.*

2. *On reaching the wall, go through a gap, then turn left to follow the signposted path towards the Grouse Inn.*

3. *At the next signpost, turn left and continue downhill through a copse. Pass through a gate and walk down to a gate at the main road (B6054) opposite the Grouse Inn.*

4. *Cross the road, turn left and walk to a stile on the right just past the pub car park. Cross the stile, then bear half-left to gateposts. Continue straight on and pass through a handgate.*

5. *Turn left, continue over a stile and straight on alongside the car park (Haywood) as signposted to Froggatt Edge. Go down and across a stream, then up to the main road.*

6. *Turn right, then cross over in a few metres and go through a handgate on the left of a white gate. Continue along this footpath for a little over 2 miles, passing above Froggatt Edge and Curbar Edge. Eventually, a handgate is reached. Go through it and take a left fork to return to the car park at Curbar Gap.*

The stones are all that is left of a burial mound or 'barrow', the softer earth mound having eroded away over the years or been crudely excavated by people in the past searching for buried treasure.

Further on, the jingling of climbing tackle will be heard. Where the cliff edge is close to the footpath — children should be adequately supervised here — climbers in their colourful wardrobe will be seen belayed (i.e. tied on to the rock) at the top of the crag 'taking in the slack' as the person on the other end climbs the route below. For a closer look at the climbs and the climbers an easy waymarked path leads down to the right and below the crags. There are many classic and difficult climbs at Froggatt Edge but there are also lots of easier and medium grade climbs of quality. This and its proximity to the road make Froggatt a very popular climbers' venue.

Refreshments

At the Grouse Inn: bar snacks, coffee, patio, family room, tables and benches outside in the summer season.

Access by bus

To the Grouse Inn only from Sheffield and Buxton (Whites), every day.

On Curbar Edge

Sir William Hill and Eyam Edge

Outline
Eyam − Sir William Hill − Nether Bretton − Bretton − Eyam.

Summary
The walk starts in the famous Derbyshire 'plague' village of Eyam, and several of the
more interesting features associated with the plague are passed en route. On leaving
Eyam, the first mile heads uphill to the summit of Sir William Hill, most of the hard
work being concentrated in the first ½ mile, which is steep. Once at the top, the
walking is on the level or in descent. There are excellent views from Sir William Hill
and from Bretton across the gritstone country to the north and the limestone plateau
to the south. A combination of well-defined footpaths, tracks and short sections of
country lane are used as the route passes through woodland, gritstone moorland and
limestone pasture amidst the countryside to the north and west of Eyam.

Attractions
Although a fuller exploration of Eyam would take half a day at least, the walk from
the car park passes some of the more interesting features. On the village green are the
well-preserved stocks once used as a punishment for minor offences against person
or property. Opposite is Eyam Hall, a fine Derbyshire manor house built by the
Wright family in 1676. Just a little further on are the 17th century 'Plague Cottages'
where the bubonic plague, known as the 'Black Death', claimed its first victims in the
village. The disease is reputed to have come to Eyam via a box of infected cloth from
London. Under the leadership of the Reverend William Mompesson the village
remained in voluntary isolation from neighbouring villages. More than two-thirds of
Eyam's inhabitants died, and many are buried in the churchyard.

   Also in the churchyard, and on your route through the village, is a fine 8th century
Saxon cross, reputedly the best example of its kind in the Midlands. The cross bears
both pagan and Christian symbols − the local Saxons were obviously hedging their
bets! Just beyond the churchyard, the walk passes by the spoil heaps of Glebe Mine,
which extracted fluorspar until 1979. On Sir William Hill, the mineral is still extracted
at the Ladywash Mine.

   The stiff climb out of the village is rewarded by extensive views both north and
south, and many distant features can be picked out. From Sir William Hill an easy
mile and a half along tracks leads through Nether Bretton, overlooking the secluded
Bretton Clough, to the 17th century Barrel Inn at Bretton. Looking southwards from
the inn one of the most striking features of the White Peak meets the eye − the
network of numerous small rectangular fields, all enclosed by limestone walls built
without the use of mortar and from stone cleared from the land over the centuries.

Continued on page 55

51

Route 9

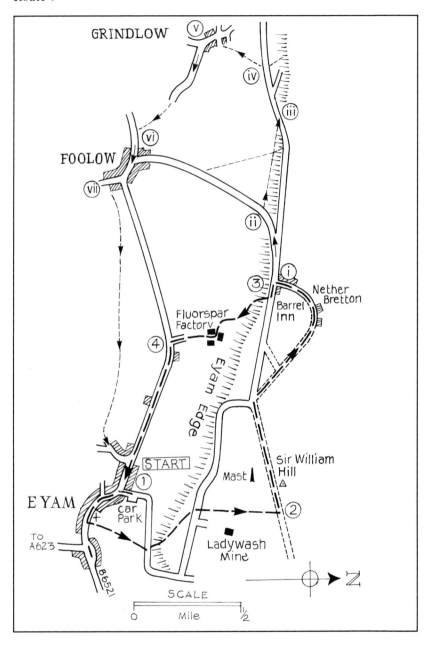

Route 9

Sir William Hill and Eyam Edge

4 miles (Longer variation 7 miles)

Start

At Eyam, which lies 4 miles north-west of Baslow on the B6521. Park in the official car park on the west side of the village (GR 216767).

Route

1. *From the car park walk to the church in the centre of the village. Go into the churchyard and continue to the right of the church alongside a wall. The footpath leads to a kissing gate which is the north entrance to the churchyard. Go through the kissing gate and keep straight on, ignoring other possibilities, to reach a stile. Cross this and continue up steeply via two further stiles to a lane. Cross the lane and the steps and stile opposite, then continue ascending even more steeply along the obvious footpath to reach another lane. Go left for a few metres to a stile on the right. Cross this and follow the path above Ladywash Mine to reach a wide, gravel track.*

2. *Turn left along the track and follow it up and over the summit of Sir William Hill and down to a junction with a road. Go straight on along the road for 100 metres, then fork right down a track. Stay on this, ignoring other possibilities. After ½ mile the track bends left and rejoins the road at Bretton.*

3. *Turn left and walk past the Barrel Inn for 100 metres to a stile and footpath sign for Eyam on the right. Cross the stile and a second stile, then bear left downhill. Cross another two stiles then enter the fluorspar factory grounds. Continue through and down to the road.*

4. *Turn left and follow the pavement back into Eyam.*

Longer variation (taking in Grindlow and Foolow)

As for 1 and 2 above to Bretton, then:

i. *Turn right along the road and in 200 metres take the left fork. Follow the road downhill for about 300 metres to a footpath on the right at a left-hand bend.*

ii. *Follow this footpath between a wall and a fence. Keep straight on at a footpath crossroads to reach a lane. (Turning left at the crossroads would lead more directly to Foolow but would involve ⅓ mile of roadwalking).*

iii. *Go left along the lane, then take a left fork. Continue along this lane for a further 200 metres to a stile and footpath on the left (Public Footpath sign).*

iv. *Cross the stile and go straight down through fields via stiles to a stile in a wall on the left. Cross this and turn right. Head for the farm track. Follow white arrows through a handgate by a wall on the left, then follow a farm track to and across a stepping stile in the right-hand corner of a small field. The stile is hidden from view until you are almost upon it. Walk past cottages to a lane. This is Grindlow.*

v. *Go left for a short distance to gain a walled track on the left (Public Footpath sign). Follow this, then a well-stiled footpath to a road.*

vi. *Turn left into Foolow, then turn right along the road signposted to Wardlow. Go as far as the last cottage on the left.*

vii. *Turn left here and walk past the front of the cottage, crossing two stiles. Continue through fields with stiles marking the way for 1¼ miles to a tarmac lane. Turn left to reach the main road, then right at the road to reach the car park.*

The old stocks at Eyam

Foolow

If the longer route is taken, field paths and footpaths fringed with wild roses and bramble lead into the tiny hamlet of Grindlow. From here, your route crosses many of those small, rectangular fields that could be seen from the Barrel Inn on its way back to Eyam. Fortunately, however, the repetitious nature of this part of the walk is broken by a visit to Foolow, a charming and picturesque village with a pond and its resident ducks, and a 14th century market cross. Foolow also has a number of interesting old cottages and a tiny chapel, and a second round of refreshments could be enjoyed at the Lazy Landlord on this rather long but attractive walk.

Refreshments
Ay Eyam – Bull's Head: bar snacks, tea and coffee, small patio planned – Rose and Crown: bar meals and snacks, tea and coffee, beer garden, patio, children's play facilities planned, cheap children's drinks and snacks, car park free to ramblers visiting pub either before or after walk – Miner's Arms: meals and bar lunches, tea and coffee, benches at the back of the pub. At Bretton – Barrel Inn: bar snacks, tea and coffee, beer garden, tables and benches at front of pub, children admitted. At Foolow – Lazy Landlord: bar lunches, tea and coffee, tables and benches on pavement in front of pub.

Access by bus
To Eyam and Foolow from Sheffield and Buxton every day (Whites), also from Chesterfield and Buxton every day (East Midland) and from Chesterfield and Manchester every day (Hulley's).

Peter Dale from Tideswell

Outline
Tideswell – Monksdale House – Peter Dale – Wheston – Tideswell.

Summary
This walk visits one of the more secluded and less frequented of the limestone dales, Peter Dale. Although it does not attain the proportions of the more spectacular dales, it does, nevertheless, possess the features of a limestone gorge, and what it lacks in size is more than compensated for by its air of tranquility. Starting at Tideswell, one of the largest White Peak villages north of the Wye, field paths lead up onto the moor to the west. From here, there are extensive views of the local countryside. A short descent along a country lane is then followed down into Peter Dale, part of which is a Nature Reserve. After walking the length of Peter Dale, the walk can be extended to include the even more remote Hay Dale, with its relics of past lead mining. Either way, the route back involves a little road-walking along lanes before picking up a track that leads across the moor once more and back down into Tideswell.

Attractions
Tideswell, so often bypassed by visitors to the Peak District, has plenty to interest the tourist and is well equipped with shops, inns and tea-shops. Its origins date back to pre-Roman times, although its name probably derives from an 8th century Saxon chieftain called Tid or Tidi. The village was an important lead mining centre for the Romans for 300 years. From the 17th to the 19th centuries lead was again mined in the immediate vicinity but on a much larger scale, and there are many relics of this era to be seen around Tideswell. The focal point of the village is undoubtedly its splendid parish church which, because of its size and its great tower, is known as "the cathedral of the Peak". Built between 1320 and 1370, the church testifies to Tideswell's importance and prosperity in bygone years.

After climbing out of Tideswell, it is worth stopping for the view over the village, which nestles comfortably in the shelter of a shallow and dry limestone valley. From the high point on the first part of the walk across the moor, there are panoramic views of the limestone plateau. Of more interest to children are the many stiles that have to be crossed as the field path cuts across the tiny fields en route. The limestone that the walls and stiles are made of is, itself, worthy of closer inspection, for the stone is made up entirely of the fossilized remains of shellfish which thrived in the tropical sea that covered this area about 350 million years ago.

A short, sharp descent leads down into Peter Dale. This is quite narrow and gorge-like with small rock buttresses and dense foliage lining the valley sides. It is also a Nature Reserve and there is a wealth of plant life in the dale, amongst which are some rare mosses and lichens. Rocky dales are also the habitat of many species of wildflower. Growing amidst the rocks you should see herb robert and stonecrop.

Further up the valley is Hay Dale, through which the longer walk passes. Here, there is evidence of lead mining, and small rock samples containing minerals may be found in the spoil heaps alongside the footpaths. In the upper part of the dale an avenue of trees provides an ideal shady spot for a picnic on a hot summer's day.

On emerging from the close confines of the dale, the openness of the remainder of the walk provides pleasant contrast and extensive views across the countryside. Whilst walking along the lanes and tracks on the way back to Tideswell, this is an ideal opportunity to investigate their borders for wild flowers. Look out for the lilac-flowered wild thyme, the cowslip and the harebell.

Refreshments
At Tideswell — Geoge Hotel: meals and bar lunches, tea and coffee, beer garden, family room — Horse and Jockey: bar lunches, coffee, beer garden — several tea-shops and two restaurants.

Access by bus
To Tideswell from Bakewell, Monday to Saturday (Hulley's), from Buxton and Sheffield, every day (Whites), from Chesterfield and Buxton, every day (East Midland), and from Manchester, Stockport and Chesterfield, every day (Hulley's).

Herb Robert. April — November (Pink)

Route 10

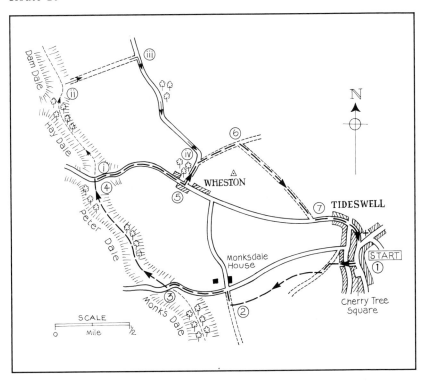

Grey Wagtail. Blue-grey above with yellow-green rump and yellow beneath

58

Route 10

Peter Dale from Tideswell

5 miles (Longer variation 7 miles)

Start

Although it is possible for a few cars to park at the junction of Peter Dale and Monk's Dale (GR 131753), unless the party requires a pub stop en route it is preferable to start in Tideswell. The walk is described from Cherry Tree Square car park, 300 metres south of the church on the west of the B6049 (GR 152755).

Route

1. *From the car park go up Sunny Bank Lane to a T-junction. Go straight across and through a stile opposite, then continue in the same direction along a field path to reach a track via a stile. Turn left at the track and, in about 100 metres, turn right over a stile. Continue through meadows with stiles clearly marking the way for just over ½ mile to a track.*

2. *Turn right and follow the track to a road, then go left and walk down the road into the dale.*

3. *Turn right into Peter Dale (Monk's Dale is to the left. Monk's Dale Nature Reserve stretches into Peter Dale). Continue through the dale for a mile to a lane.*

4. *Turn right and walk uphill into Wheston, to where a road joins on the left.*

5. *Turn left here and follow the road past a small wood on the left to where a track joins on the right 100 metres further on. Follow this track to a junction with another track coming from the right.*

6. *Turn right along this track and follow it for ¾ mile to reach a road.*

7. *Turn left along the road and walk into Tideswell, bearing right to the car park.*

Longer variation (Taking in Hay Dale) *As for 1 to 3 above, then:*

i. *Turn right and walk 50 metres to a stile on the left. Cross this and continue up Hay Dale for about ½ mile to a stile.*

ii. *After crossing the stile, turn right along the track and follow it uphill to a road.*

iii. *Turn right at the road. Follow it for ¾ mile to a point where a track joins on the left shortly after a right-hand bend.*

iv. *Turn left. This is the first track mentioned in 5. Continue as for 5 to 7 above.*

Hathersage Moor, Bole Hill and Derwent Valley

Outline
Hathersage − Scraperlow − Mitchell Field − Millstone Edge − Bole Hill − Padley − Leadmill − Hathersage.

Summary
A first rate walk combining gritstone moor, woodland and riverside. The first mile and a half is uphill and steep in parts but once this is accomplished, the remainder is on the level or downhill! From the moor there are exceptionally good views of the Hope Valley and its surrounding hills and moors. En route, the walk passes through the old quarry workings of Millstone Edge and Bole Hill, and there are various interesting relics to see and features to explore. Also, a visit to the 14th century Padley Chapel could be included. Footpaths and tracks are followed throughout.

Attractions
Hathersage has several interesting features and curiosities which could be explored after the walk (see Route 12). On leaving the village, a steep ascent with gradually improving views of the Hope Valley leads through woodland to the open, gritstone moorland east of Hathersage. The highest point on the walk is reached early on and, with the crags of Higger Tor as a backdrop, is a fitting place to stop and rest and take in the surroundings. From this fine spot, the footpath traverses the flanks of Hathersage Moor just below the rocks of Winyards Nick and Over Owler Tor. A footpath runs along the top of the rocks, and this could be followed as an alternative to the lower level path, which would be rejoined a little further on.

The next major feature is Millstone Edge. If the more adventurous route through the spoil heaps of the former quarry is taken, it is worth pausing to watch climbers making progress, or otherwise, up the sheer cliffs and slabs of the quarried Edge, which is higher than 100 feet in places. Although Millstone Edge was quarried mainly for building stone, Peakland sandstone was used to make high quality millstones from the 14th to the mid-19th century. Hence, this type of sandstone has become known as Millstone Grit. After crossing the busy A625, you will see beside the wide former quarry track rows of millstones fashioned from stone from Bole Hill quarry. In the second half of the 19th century, the rapid introduction and adoption of the more efficient rollers to mill flour explains why the millstones were abandoned and the industry ceased. On the way down to Padley, the overgrown Bole Hill quarry and vaious relics can be explored. In this area the large and ferocious wood ants have built massive nets. As you descend through the woods below the quarry, keep a lookout for nuthatch and tree-creeper.

On reaching Padley, refreshments can be had at Grindleford Station Cafe. And if you sit outside, you might see a train emerge from the Totley Tunnel, which was built towards the end of the last century by the Midland Railway to provide a more direct link between Sheffield and Manchester.

Not far from the station is Padley Chapel, all that remains of the 14th-15th century manor house of Padley Hall. The hall belonged to the Eyre family, who were staunchly Roman Catholic. In 1588, when religious intolerance was rife in England, the Earl of Shrewsbury raided Padley Chapel and captured two Jesuit priests found hiding there. They were taken to Derby, where they were brought to trial and, later, hung, drawn and quartered and their heads stuck on poles for public display.

On the last leg of the walk, the route passes through a pleasant piece of wilderness known as Coppice Wood, after which the riverside footpath is followed to Leadmill. You are likely to spot dippers on this stretch. Less easily seen is the spotted flycatcher, which darts from its perch amongst riverside trees to catch insects.

Refreshments

At Hathersage Booths (shorter walk) − Millstone Inn: bar meals, tables and benches outside, tea and coffee. At Padley − Grindleford Station Cafe. At Leadmill − The Plough Inn: meals and bar snacks, tea and coffee, beer garden. At Hathersage − Scotsman's Pack Inn: meals and bar snacks, tea and coffee, beer garden, children admitted. − Longland's (cafe) and a tea-shop.

Access by bus

Hathersage is well-served by bus from Sheffield, Chesterfield, Matlock, Bakewell, Buxton, Castleton (SYT, East Midland, Hulley's and White's). Also accessible by train from Manchester, New Mills and Sheffield.

North Lees Hall

Route 11

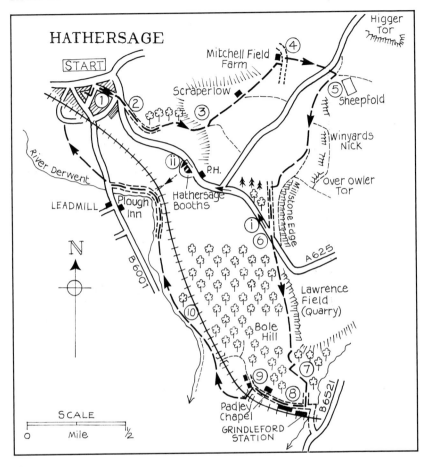

HATHERSAGE

START

Higger Tor

Mitchell Field Farm

Scraperlow

Sheepfold

Winyards Nick

Over Owler Tor

River Derwent

P.H.

Hathersage Booths

LEADMILL

Plough Inn

Millstone Edge

A625

N

Lawrence Field (Quarry)

Bole Hill

B6001

Padley Chapel

GRINDLEFORD STATION

B6521

SCALE

0   Mile   ½

Route 11

Hathersage Moor, Bole Hill and Derwent Valley   6 miles (Shorter variation 4 miles)

Start

At Hathersage. The walk is described from the pay and display car park (GR 231814).

Route

1. *With your back to the car park, turn left and follow the street round a right-hand corner and up to a junction. Turn right along the main road (A625) in the direction of Sheffield, and walk uphill for 200 metres as far as a narrow lane on the left that joins the main road near a bus stop.*

2. *Cross the road and go up the narrow lane (Public Footpath sign). Continue uphill steeply. The tarmac lane becomes a track which ends at a stile and fence. Cross the stile, then follow either of two footpaths that bear right uphill — the higher level one is the easier of the two. Continue to a stile.*

3. *After crossing this stile,* **ignore the path and stile directly ahead** *and, instead, fork left to a stile next to a wall. Continue with the wall on the left, passing the impressive private residence at Scraperlow. Follow the footpath signposted to Mitchell Field Farm. Just before reaching the farm, cross two stiles, then go left along the drive as signposted for a few metres to another signpost.*

4. *Turn right here and walk uphill through fields to a road. The last 100 metres is very steep. Cross the road and ascend the steps then follow the wall on the right to join a footpath.*

5. *Turn right along this. In just under ½ mile follow the right fork down to a stile (yellow arrow). Cross the stile and, after a few metres, descend to a former quarry track on the right. Turn left along this and follow it to the main road (A625). (An alternative and more adventurous route for those who enjoy scrambling takes a higher-level path, difficult in places, below the quarried cliffs of Millstone Edge. At the road, turn right to reach the lower track of the easier route. NB A wary eye should be kept on youngsters in the vicinity of the quarry.)*

6. *Cross the road, go through a handgate and down steps (signposted Bole Hill) and continue along a wide straight grassy track. Where it ends, follow the well-used footpath that zigzags down old spoil heaps and embankments, then bears left down through trees to a handgate.*

7. *Go through the gate and past waterworks property to a gate and stile on the right.*

63

Go through the gate and down an unsurfaced road to a T-junction with another unsurfaced road. This is Padley. (200 metres to the left is Grindleford Station cafe.)

8. Turn right and walk along the unsurfaced road past houses. Continue past Padley Chapel and across a cattle grid.

9. Immediately after the cattle grid, turn left, go through a gate and cross a railway bridge. Keep straight on with a wall on the left, ignoring a left fork at a gap in the wall, as far as a gateway with footpath sign for Leadmill just to the right of it. Continue as signposted alongside the wall. The path bears half-right towards a second railway bridge. Do not cross the bridge. Instead, continue through a handgate leading into Coppice Wood (signposted). Follow the footpath down through the wood to the riverside footpath.

10. Turn right along this and follow it for 1½ miles to reach a main road (B6001). (The Plough Inn is 250 metres to the left on the other side of the bridge.) Cross the road to a stile opposite. Continue straight on along the well-used footpath. Where it meets a lane, go left to explore Hathersage or right for a more direct route back to the car park. NB In or after wet weather, the footpath from Leadmill becomes very muddy and can be avoided by walking along the pavement alongside the B6001 back into Hathersage.

Shorter variation

As for 1 to 5 above to the A625, then:

i. Turn right and walk downhill on the pavement for about ½ mile to Hathersage Booths and The Millstone Inn. 150 metres further on and at the far end of the last building on the left is a drive with a Public Footpath sign.

ii. Go down this drive, cross a stile and continue downhill via stiles to the railway. Cross it via a footbridge and turn right along the riverside footpath. Continue as for 10 above.

8th Century Saxon cross, Eyam churchyard (Route 9).

High Neb and Sheepwash Bank

Outline

Hathersage − North Lees − High Neb − Dennis Knoll − Green's House − Hathersage.

Summary

From low-lying Hathersage in the Hope Valley, tracks and footpaths lead for 1000 feet (about 300 metres) uphill via pastures, woodland, and open country to Stanage Edge and High Neb. Although the first half of the ascent is gradual, the second half is fairly steep and strenuous. Once on Stanage Edge, however, the way back is all downhill. A shorter variation cuts the amount of ascent down by a third and, at the same time, takes in all the features of the wilder section of the walk. Footpaths and tracks are followed throughout. The section along the top of Stanage Edge is particularly exposed though short.

Attractions

En route out of the busy little town of Hathersage, the walk passes through the churchyard of Hathersage Parish Church. On its southeast side is a large grave marked by an ancient and heavily pruned yew tree. The inscription on the headstone is: "Here lies buried Little John, the friend and lieutenant of Robin Hood". It also says that he died in a cottage to the east of the churchyard. Whether Robin Hood existed or not, tradition has it that a giant of a man called John Little lived in the village in the 13th century. And in those times, the Forest of Sherwood stretched well into this part of Derbyshire.

The church is 14th century and has some famous brasses, and the nearby vicarage is where Charlotte Brontë stayed in 1845. Just beyond the church, the footpath taken follows the edge of a circular earthwork known as Camp Green. This is thought to have been constructed in the early 10th century by Danes during one of the invasions into Saxon Peakland.

Another mile further on up the valley is North Lees Hall, a 16th century tower house that belonged to the Eyre family. The first member of the Eyre family to arrive on British soil was a Norman invader who is reputed to have fought alongside William the Conqueror at the Battle of Hastings. An interesting and possibly factual account of how the name 'Eyre' came about can be read at the Eyre Arms in Hassop. Moving on to the 19th century, it is generally regarded that North Lees Hall made a great impression on Charlotte Brontë, who used it and the family name in her novel "Jane Eyre".

A steady climb leads up through woodland from the old hall to the road that runs along the foot of Stanage Edge and to the Mountain Rescue Post, where a stretcher and various other items of first aid equipment are stored in the event of accident on the rocks above. A rest is in order here or, even better, at the picnic table on the edge of Hollin Bank car park just a short distance away.

The remaining uphill section leads through a plantation of conifers then along a paved footpath constructed for packhorses and their jaggers passing between Hathersage and Sheffield. To the right of the footpath there are boulders of various sizes that have broken away from the cliffs of Stanage Edge. Some of these are suitable for children to explore and climb but grown-ups should keep a watchful eye on their antics hereabouts.

Stanage Edge itself is a rock-climber's paradise. The rock is firm, quick to dry, and there is plenty of it. Walking along the top of Stanage towards High Neb, with the slope below the Edge dropping steeply away, one can also appreciate the appeal to climbers of this lofty situation, yet one which is so easily accessible from the road.

After reaching the triangulation pillar at High Neb (height 458 metres), find an easy way down to watch climbers attempting some of the more intimidating routes here. As on other Derbyshire crags, the legendary Joe Brown left his mark at High Neb by scaling free of aid the large overhanging roof known as Quietus.

On the way back, just to the east of the plantation at Dennis Knoll, is a justly popular picnic spot, shown on the map as Sheepwash Bank. Here, there is a little, tumbling stream, and the level area shows evidence of an ancient settlement and field system — a place to relax and to ponder the surroundings before the descent to Hathersage.

Refreshments

At Hathersage — Scotsman's Pack: meals and bar snacks, tea and coffee, beer garden, children admitted — Longland's Cafe and a tea-shop.

Access by bus

Hathersage is well-served by bus from Sheffield, Matlock, Bakewell, Buxton, Castleton (SYT, East Midland, Hulley's and White's). Also accessible by train from Manchester, New Mills and Sheffield.

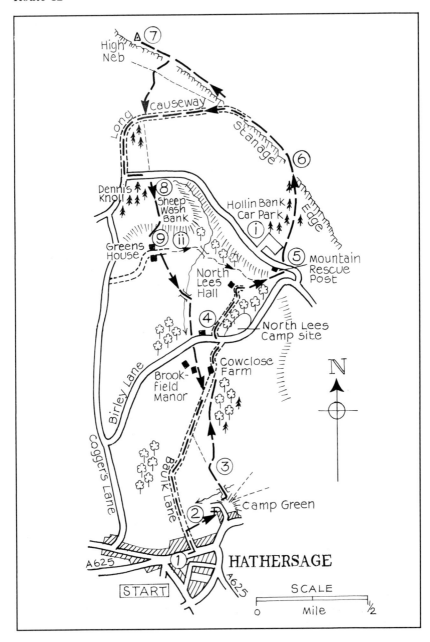

Route 12

High Neb and Sheepwash Bank

6 miles (Shorter variation 3 miles)

Start

At Hathersage. The walk is described from the pay and display car park (GR 231814). It could also be started at Hollin Bank car park on the unclassified road below Stanage Edge (GR 237837).

Route

1. *On the opposite side of the car park to the entrance go through a stile and past the Methodist Church to reach the main road (A625). Cross the road, turn right behind the bank up Besom Lane, then turn left along a track (Baulk Lane). Continue for 100 metres to the footpath on the right signposted to the church.*

2. *Follow this to and through the churchyard – Little John's Grave is to the right – and through the lychgate. Turn left along a lane. In a few metres go straight ahead over a stile. Follow the footpath around the embankment of Camp Green for about **50 metres only**, then go down to the left to cross a stile and a stream. Continue straight on with a fence on the left to the end of the field only.*

3. *Bear half-right here to a stile in a fence, then continue in the same direction to join a more obvious footpath. Go left along this and keep straight on, keeping a hedge on the left. After passing through a farm gate (Cowclose Farm), follow the footpath round to the right of the farm buildings. Go through a handgate, join a track and continue to a road. (A sign indicates the track is private but it is a right of way.)*

4. *Go left for a few metres, then right up the drive to North Lees Hall. Continue as signposted past the Hall, then up through a wood to a road.*

5. *Turn left, then bear right along a grassy footpath opposite the building housing the Mountain Rescue Kit. Follow this, and the paved packhorse route, to the top of Stanage Edge.*

6. *Go left along Stanage Edge and stay on the footpath above the cliffs until you reach the triangulation pillar at High Neb. (A shorter variation missing out High Neb follows the Long Causeway, the obvious track leading off the Edge – to reach the plantation at Dennis Knoll.)*

7. *Retrace your steps beyond the cliff at High Neb for a short distance then head down to join the track (Long Causeway) below via an obvious footpath and a stile. Follow the track downhill to its junction with the road. Turn left and walk to the*

far side of the plantation on the right (Dennis Knoll).

8. *Turn right (signposted to Green's House) and continue alongside the plantation. Follow the path downhill to Green's House.*

9. *After a gate turn left to pass between the house and a building on the left. Go through a gate and turn right immediately along an enclosed footpath. After a handgate, continue straight on downhill and through another handgate. Cross a footbridge and bear right to reach a road. Cross this, then follow the signposted path around to the left of Brookfield Manor. On reaching a track, go right and follow the track all the way back into Hathersage.*

Shorter variation

    This walk starts and finishes at Hollin Bank car park, at 5 above, on the road that runs below and parallel to Stanage Edge (GR 237837). The road is accessible via Cogger's Lane and Birley Lane from Hathersage, as shown on the map.

i. *From the car park walk away from the entrance to join the well-used footpath that ascends the hillside. Continue as for 5 to 8 above to Green's House. Pass between the buildings and through a gate.*

ii. *Instead of turning right along the enclosed footpath, keep straight on along an old and grassy walled track. Continue through a handgate, then bear half-right to cross a stile. Head for another gate, then follow the farm track down to a ford next to ruins. Cross the stepping stones and continue uphill along the winding track as signposted. After a stile to the left of a gate, keep straight on along a footpath to join another path at a gate/stile. Turn left here and continue up to a road, then turn left to reach the car park at Hollin Bank, passing the Mountain Rescue Post en route.*

Harebell. July—October (Blue)

70

Bradwell — on the way out of the village

Bradwell Edge and Abney Moor

Outline
Bradwell — Bradwell Edge — Abney Moor — Great Hucklow —
Hazlebadge Hall — Bradwell.

Summary
A varied walk with good views and plenty of interest. From Bradwell, the route
begins with a short but strenuous climb up to the top of Bradwell Edge to the east of
the village. A level stretch of moorland follows after which the Gliding Club on
Abney Moor is passed. A short descent from here leads down to the little village of
Great Hucklow with its friendly inn and its past association with lead mining, then
a gradual descent back to Bradwell is made across the limestone terrain below
Bradwell Edge. Footpaths and tracks are followed throughout except for 200 metres
alongside the main road south of Bradwell.

Attractions
The older part of Bradwell is very quaint, with narrow lanes and alleys and 17th and
18th century cottages clustered along the lower slopes of the valley. The village grew
as a mining community and, unlike its neighbour, Castleton, it has not developed as
a tourist centre. However, it does have a show cave, Bagshawe Cavern, which is well
worth a visit. It is half a mile in length and has many interesting features.

   The sighting of rabbits on the stiff climb to the top of Bradwell Edge provides
distraction on the way up but the biggest reward is the fine view across the Hope
Valley to Lose Hill and Back Tor. Bradwell Edge is also a launching site for hang-
gliders and paragliders, who use this spot because of the strong updraught that is
characteristic of such edges. Watching these people launch provides another excuse
to stop and take a proper rest before continuing the walk.

   Leaving the aerial interest behind for a while, the walk across Abney Moor
provides contrast with the hill-climb. The grass, gorse and bracken of the valley
slopes are replaced by the moor grasses, mat grass and cotton grass which grow
readily on the peaty soils of the sandstone moorland.

   On the southwest corner of Abney Moor is the cultivated airstrip of the Derbyshire
and Lancashire Gliding Club, where you can watch gliders being launched by winch.
Nearby Burr's Mount (shown on the accompanying map), which forms the southern
boundary of the gliding club, has been identified as the site of an Iron Age hill-fort.
The word 'burr' derives from the Old English 'burh', meaning a fortification.

   A short descent from this point through woodland leads to Great Hucklow.
Mentioned in the Domesday Survey, the village was an established settlement in the
11th century. It is probable that lead was mined here at that time, and this continued
until the end of the 19th century. To the right of the track leading out of the village
are a few buildings that are the remains of Mill Dam Mine, and a building in the

village now occupied by Hucklow Players Theatre was once a lead smelting mill. Nowadays, the lead mining has been replaced by the mining of fluorspar, a mineral used in the chemical and steel industries.

From Great Hucklow, tracks and field paths lead down towards Bradwell, passing Hazlebadge Hall on the way. This is one of several 16th century houses in the area, other examples being Offerton Hall and Highlow Hall to the east.

Refreshments
At Great Hucklow – Queen Anne: pub food on Sundays only, tea and coffee, beer garden, family room, hiking boots to be left in porch but walkers welcome. At Bradwell – Lyndale Cafe.

Access by bus
To Bradwell from Sheffield and Castleton every day (SYT, Hulley's), and from Buxton and Chesterfield, summer Sundays and Bank Holiday Mondays only (Hulley's).

17th Century relics, Bradwell

73

Route 13

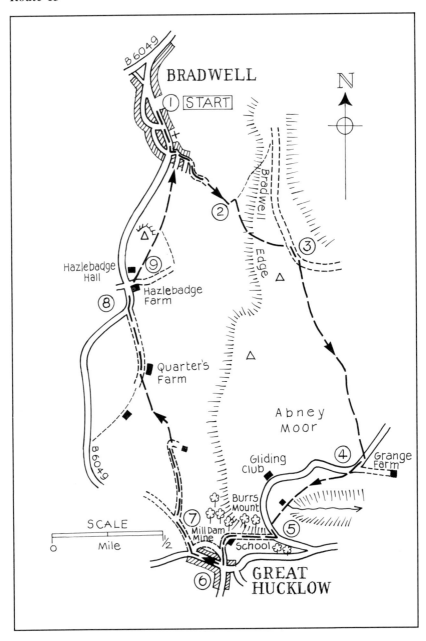

Route 13

Bradwell Edge and Abney Moor4¾ miles

Start

At Bradwell, on the B6049 south of the A625 between Castleton and Hathersage. Park in the public car park behind Food Fair Supermarket in the centre of the village (GR 173814).

Route

1. *With your back to the car park turn left along the road. Continue past the church, then fork left along Church Street. Go up the steps on the left of Clematis Cottage and keep straight on along Bessie Lane. In a few metres take a left fork, then follow the lane uphill (a public footpath sign points the way.) The lane soon degenerates into a track. Continue over a stile. Follow the steepening footpath uphill to a fork by an old keyhole stile. The main footpath goes left here.* **Do not follow it.**

2. *Branch right here and continue steeply uphill with a fence/wall on the right. At the top of the hill cross a stone stile. Continue in the same direction, pass through a squeeze stile, and cross a third stile (stepping stile) to join a track.*

3. *Turn right along the track and go through a gate. After 100 metres leave the track and fork right over a wooden stile. Continue along the moorland footpath for a mile to join a road after a stile.*

4. *Turn right at the road.* **Either** *follow the road for just over ½ mile, passing the Gliding club, to reach a wood on the right.* **Or,** *to avoid roadwalking, cross a stile on the left about 100 metres along the road − a farm lane joins at the same point. Aim for the left-hand corner of the field and a stile. Cross it, then descend to cross a stream, after which you go up to and across a stile. Carry on in the same direction, then drop down to cross a stile on the left of an isolated building. Go uphill via the stiled footpath to rejoin the road, then go left to the wood.*

5. *Fork right along a footpath, then turn right to follow a track down through the wood. Continue past a school and join the road at Great Hucklow.*

6. *Turn right, continue past the Queen Anne, then turn right down a track (Public Footpath sign). Continue to a fork in 200 metres.*

7. *Take the right fork through a gate (signposted). Continue straight on past a building. Where the track bends, keep straight on as signposted and cross a stile. Keep close to the wall on the right, avoiding a muddy section by a wide sweep to the left. Cross another stile, bear half-left, then walk with a fence on the right. Bear right with the fence but avoid the area of landfill by skirting it* **on the left.** *Continue*

to a wooden stile. Cross it and descend to farm buildings (Quarter's Farm). Turn right and pass in front of the farm. Follow the farm road down to a main road (B6049).

8. *Turn right at the road. Follow this WITH CAUTION to the farm on the right (Hazlebadge Farm). Turn right along a footpath that goes behind the farm buildings (signposted to Bradwell). Continue to a track via a stile, then go through a gate.*

9. *Immediately after the gate, bear left off the track up a field. Head for the right-hand fence and keep it on the right as you continue straight on. The fieldpath passes just to the right of the highest point, which is a tumulus, then becomes a more obvious footpath as it descends towards Bradwell. Continue across a stile just left of a bungalow, then keep straight on into Bradwell and the car park.*

Looking down Cave Dale towards Peveril Castle

76

Cave Dale and Windy Knoll

Outline

Castleton − Cave Dale − Hurdlow − Windy Knoll − Odin Mine − Castleton.

Summary

Whilst Castleton and Winnat's Pass have throngs of tourists, the walk described keeps well away from the busier spots yet visits some of the most spectacular features in the area around the village. Leaving Castleton, a footpath is followed through the impressive Cave Dale and up onto the moor to the southwest of the village. A track is then followed to Windy Knoll and its cave, after which the descent begins. This passes the Blue John Mine, a visit to which could be included en route, then follows the old and dramatically subsided road below Mam Tor, the 'shivering mountain'. This leads round to Odin Mine, an old lead mine with a crushing circle that is still intact. From here a footpath through fields is followed back into Castleton.

Attractions

Castleton, as its name implies, owes its origins to the castle, whose construction began soon after the Norman Conquest by William Peveril, an illegitimate son of the conqueror. The impressive stone keep was erected by Henry II in 1176. The castle's main use was that of a hunting lodge and was the residence of the Keeper of the Royal Forest of the High Peak. Castleton is, perhaps, most famous for its four show caves and the semi-precious Blue John stone still extracted from two of these. All the caves are worth visiting, especially on a wet day when such a visit could be combined with a tour of Castleton's curiosities and museums.

The route out of the village goes via Cave Dale, from which there are good views of the castle keep on its lofty perch above limestone cliffs. Cave Dale is spectacular in its lower reaches, where the cliffs are highest. It is thought its formation is the result of the passage of torrents through the limestone towards the end of the last Ice Age, when there was much more surface water than there is today.

On emerging from the narrow confines of Cave Dale, tracks lead across a limestone moor to the aptly named Windy Knoll. Here, and well concealed from the road and the car park nearby, is a shallow but large cave from which various bones have been excavated of animals that were hunted by Stone Age nomads in the area. On a windless day, Windy Knoll would be a choice spot for a picnic.

A little further on is the Blue John Mine, which is open all year round, and a visit could easily be included on the itinerary. Blue John is a corruption of the French 'bleu-jeune', meaning blue-yellow, and accurately describes the colour of this semi-precious stone. Working the Blue John stone dates from the mid-18th century. Small quantities are still mined to make jewellery and various ornaments.

Continued on page 81

77

Route 14

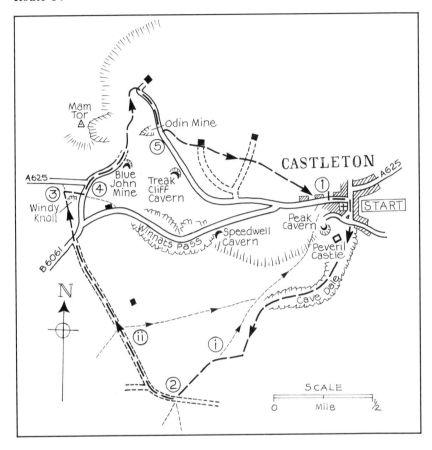

Route 14

Cave Dale and Windy Knoll

5 miles (Shorter variations 3½ miles and 2½ miles)

Start

At Castleton. The walk is described from the car park in the village (GR 149830).

Route

1. *From the car park walk up the road and past the shops to the sharp left-hand bend. Turn right by the Nag's Head along Back Street. Walk up to the Market Place, fork left along a minor road, then turn right in a few metres to enter Cave Dale (signposted). Go through the gate and follow the footpath up through the dale. After about a mile, at the third gate, the path bends right. After another gate, a footpath joins from the right. Continue, bearing half-left across a field, to reach a well-used track via gates/stiles.*

2. *Go right along the track, forking right in a short distance. Continue over a stile on the right of a gate, then keep straight on to reach a road (B6061). Cross the road to a stile by a gate. Cross the stile and follow the path to a point before the wall and road ahead where footpaths join from the right.*

3. *Turn right here to reach Windy Knoll Cave. Keep straight on past it and walk downhill to reach the B6061 by a stile.*

4. *Turn left and walk alongside the road for a few metres, then keep straight on as signposted for the Blue John Mine. Continue past the entrance to the mine to a turning circle. Cross a stile and walk down the buckled remains of the old road. Follow this round to the right to Odin Mine (signposted), which is on the right of the road.*

5. *Continue for a few metres along the road, then turn left to cross a wooden stile. Go down to and past the old ore-crushing circle, then cross a footbridge and continue along the obvious footpath. After crossing several stiles a farm track is reached with a farmyard to the left. Continue straight on across the track, through a keyhole stile and alongside a stream. Follow the well-marked footpath back into Castleton, crossing several more stiles and another farm track en route.*

Shorter variations

i. *2½ miles. As for 1 above to where the footpath joins from the right, then turn right here and follow this footpath back down to Castleton crossing stiles en route.*

ii. **3½ miles.** *As for 1 and 2 above as far as the stile on the right of a gate. Instead of keeping straight on to reach the B6061, after crossing the stile, turn right immediately to cross another (signposted Castleton). Follow the field path using stiles to guide the way. Bear left at a junction with another footpath and continue the descent to Castleton.*

The start of Peter Dale, though the sign says otherwise!

Beyond the Blue John Mine the route leaves the limestone for a while and enters shale country. The shales that have been eroded from, and caused the landslips on, the flanks of Mam Tor can be clearly seen and investigated on the left of the old road. The road, itself, which was closed in 1979, will provide great entertainment to youngsters, since it is buckled and collapsed and resembles an earthquake zone.

On re-entering the limestone country, you soon arrive at Odin Mine, which was worked for lead from the 17th century through till the last. However, the mine should not be entered since the workings are dangerous. On the opposite side of the road, and en route, is the crushing circle. Here, lead ore was heaped on the cast-iron track, then crushed by the large millstone − still there − which was rolled around a pivot by a horse.

From Odin Mine, the way back to Castleton is along a fieldpath. Some of the stone stiles demand a close inspection, since they are crammed with easily discernible fossils well polished by a multitude of feet over the years.

Refreshments
At Blue John Mine − A tea-shop. At Castleton − Several cafes/tea/coffee shops − The Peak Hotel: meals and bar snacks, tea and coffee, beer garden, children's/games room.

Access by bus
Castleton is well-served by bus from Sheffield (SYT, Hulley's), Buxton (Hulley's, Andrew's), Derby and Matlock (East Midland), and from Bakewell (Hulley's).

Spotted Flycatcher.
Mousey grey-brown with paler underparts and dark streaks on head and breast

81

Crook Hill and Ladybower

Outline

Ashopton Viaduct — Crookhill Farm — Bridge-end Pasture — Fairholmes —
Ashopton Viaduct.

Summary

A fine walk with beautiful and panoramic views of the Derwent Valley and the
surrounding ridges and moors. The route is described from Ashopton Viaduct but
could equally well be started at Fairholmes below the Derwent Dam. A gradual ascent
over 1½ miles of around 600 feet/200 metres is made through pastures to the ridge
separating the Derwent and Woodlands Valleys. After following the ridge, a descent
is made through forest to the Derwent Dam and refreshments at Fairholmes. The last
leg follows the 'lakeside' back to the viaduct. Both variations visit Lockerbrook
Heights above the forest to the west of the Derwent Dam and are worthy inclusions.

Attractions

On climbing out of the valley, the route passes through pastureland that was once the
possession of Welbeck Abbey. At the close of the 12th century, the land that separates
the two arms of Ladybower was given to the abbot of Welbeck by John, Richard I's
brother. Since then, the pastures have been devoted to sheep farming. This would
account for the lawn-like appearance of the hillsides and hilltop around Bridge-end
Pastures. From this point and further along the ridge, there are outstanding views. At
different times you will see the reservoirs of both the Woodlands and Derwent
Valleys, Win Hill, Mam Tor and the great bulk of Kinder Scout to the west. To the
east and southeast Derwent Edge and the continuation of the escarpment southwards
can be picked out.

From this lofty position, an old packhorse track is followed down through the
forest which clothes the eastern flanks of the ridge. The trees are primarily but not
all coniferous and the birdlife is both interesting and varied. With patience you may
see goldcrests, and with a lot of luck you may catch a glimpse of the rare goshawk.
The spruce and larch woodland is also home to the native red squirrels that have
managed to survive here so far.

A walk along the 'lakeside' footpath brings you to Fairholmes, where there is an
information centre as well as a shop that sells teas and the usual refreshments. There
is also cycle hire, and a fit party might wish to include a short bike ride on their
itinerary! Not far from the car park is the impressive Derwent Dam. Built of local
millstone grit, it blends perfectly with its surroundings. The building of the Howden
Dam, 1½ miles further up the valley, began in 1901 and was completed in 1916. The
temporary village of Birchinlee, otherwise known as 'Tin Town', was constructed for
the navvies who were working on the dams. It was sited on the west side of the valley

midway between the two dams. The Derwent dam was used during the Second World War by crews from the famous Dambusters Squadron to practice low level flying in preparation for the raid on the Ruhr dams in Germany. There is a small information centre in the western tower of the Derwent Dam describing the epic raid.

Work on the Ladybower Dam began in 1935 and was completed in 1945. In creating this third reservoir, two villages, Derwent and Ashopton, had to be sacrificed. Derwent village was situated where Mill Brook would have joined the River Derwent (see accompanying map). Mill Brook is crossed on the way back alongside Ladybower. In 1976, when the reservoir was particularly low, it was possible to walk amongst the ruins of Derwent village. Ashopton was situated just south of the viaduct. Many of the villagers and farmers were rehoused on the purpose-built estate at Yorkshire Bridge, whilst others resettled in other Peakland communities.

Refreshments
At Fairholmes − shop selling hot and cold drinks and other refreshments.

Access by bus
To Ladybower and Fairholmes from Chesterfield, Sheffield and Castleton every day (Chesterfield Transport − Countybus Service).

Ladybower Reservoir

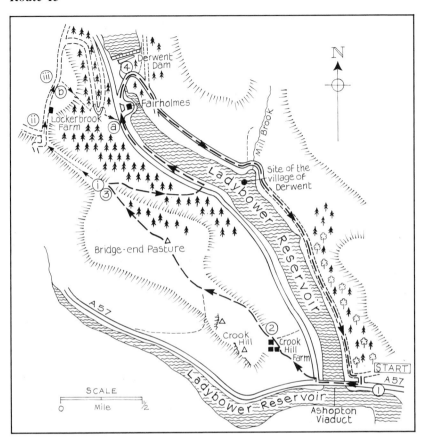

Curlew.
Pale brown with darker streaks. White rump and belly with dark bars. Curved bill

Route 15

Crook Hill and Ladybower

7½ miles (Shorter variation 2¾ miles).

Start

At Ashopton Viaduct on the A57 above Ladybower Reservoir. Park in the official layby to the east of the viaduct and about ¼ mile west of the junction of the A6013 with the A57 (GR 197864). The walk could also be started at Fairholmes car park – as does the shorter variation – situated below the Derwent Dam in the Derwent Valley (GR 173893).

Route

1. *Walk across the viaduct, turn right along the road on the far (west) side, then cross the road in a few metres to a handgate. Go through this and follow the field path as it bears right uphill towards Crookhill Farm. Go through a gate and acros another field, then cross a ladder stile. From here, follow the "National Trust Footpath Avoiding Farmyard". This passes through a gate on the right, then bears left to a handgate on the right of a large barn. Go through this and another handgate on the other side of a track. Continue in the same general direction across a field to a gate on the left.*

2. *Go through the gate and turn right along a bridleway. Continue through a bridleway gate by a signpost and straight on, via another gate, to crest the hilltop of Bridge-end Pasture. The footpath soon comes up alongside a large plantation and follows the perimeter fence along the ridge. Follow this to a stile.*

3. *Turn right here and walk down through the plantation along an old packhorse route. On reaching the road next to Bridge End car park, cross it and go left along the concessionary footpath (signposted). When it joins the road further on, continue along the pavement to Fairholmes.*

4. *Continue through the car park and take the road that passes below the dam. Follow it round to the east side of the reservoir and stay on it all the way back to the start (about 2½ miles from Fairholmes).*

Variation. Taking in Lockerbrook Heights before descending to Fairholmes via the Forest Walk (7½ miles)

As for 1 and 2 above to the stile.

i. *Instead of turning right at this point, continue over another stile straight ahead and alongside the plantation as before for a further ½ mile, where the footpath joins a track. Bear right to a junction with another track in a few metres.*

ii. *Bear right along this and walk past Lockerbrook Farm. Continue for another 300 metres to a stile on the right.**

iii. *Cross this and continue downhill to another stile. Follow the footpath as it bears right, then left down through the forest. On reaching a gravel forest track, turn right and follow it downhill round a left-hand bend, then turn right off the track and follow the Forest Walk down to Fairholmes. Continue as for 4 above.*

*(If the footpath to Fairholmes is temporarily closed due to forestry work, continue along the old track for a further ¼ mile to a gate on the right with a sign that says "Footpath for walkers only". Go down the forestry track all the way to the road just north of Derwent Dam, then turn right and walk down to Fairholmes.)

Shorter variation. START at Fairholmes and taking in Lockerbrook Heights (2¾ miles)

a. *Go back to the road from the car park. Cross it and follow the Forest Walk footpath for Lockerbrook up through the forest. ** On joining a gravel forest track, follow it uphill and round a right-hand bend, then turn left, as signposted, along the continuation of the Forest Walk footpath. Continue via stiles to reach an old track.*

b. *Turn left and walk past Lockerbrook Farm. Continue to a fork in the track at a bend. Take the left fork, then turn left off this straight away to follow a footpath alongside the top edge of the plantation on the left. Continue to a stile about ½ mile from where you left the track, then turn left and walk down through the forest along an old packhorse route. Continue as for 3 above back to Fairholmes. **(If this footpath is temporarily closed due to forest work, go right along the road and up past the Derwent Dam for a short distance to the start of a forest track on the left which is also a Concessionary Footpath. Follow the track all the way to where it ends at a gate at the top edge of the forest. From here, go left along an old track and continue as for b above.)*

The site of the submerged village of Derwent with Pike Low in the background

Hancock Wood and Pike Low

Outline

Fairholmes – Hancock Wood – Pike Low – Ladybower – Fairholmes.

Summary

A good introduction to fell walking in a beautiful part of the Peak District. This walk starts at the Derwent Dam at Fairholmes. After climbing to the east side of the dam, an easy stroll through woodland alongside Derwent Reservoir is followed by a strenuous, albeit short, climb up the steep eastern flanking hillside – in a little over ¼ mile the footpath ascends 140 metres (about 430 feet). From this point, a footpath leads uphill more gradually for another ¼ mile, then levels out before descending once more to the valley and Ladybower Reservoir. A tarmac lane is followed back to Fairholmes. There are stunning views of the Derwent Valley, Derwent Edge and surrounding moorland.

Attractions

Immediately on starting the walk, the huge Derwent Dam with its castle-like stone towers forms an impressive sight for children and adults alike, especially if the Derwent Reservoir is full and water is cascading over the dam wall. After seeing the dam from below, and since the walk leads up to the eastern side of Derwent Reservoir, the dam can then be viewed from above.

From here, a pleasant and picturesque stroll along the lakeside forest track leads to the footpath that climbs through Hancock Wood and out of the valley by the aptly named Walker's Clough. A 'clough' is a stream valley with remnant woodland. In the damper, more shaded parts of these moorland cloughs several interesting plant species can often be found, amongst which is the common butterwort.

Coming out of the woodland, the footpath zigzags steeply up through bracken to a footpath crossroads. On the way up this section, you are likely to see wild flowers bordering the path. Look out for the yellow-petalled tormentil. Just to the left of the footpath crossroads are the ruins of Bamford House, a derelict farmstead abandoned early this century which can be explored and provides a good excuse for a rest. It is also an ideal spot to absorb the splendid surroundings.

The bracken gives way to moorland grasses at this height but further along the walk towards Pike Low heather is predominant. Although heather grows on these moors naturally, what you see is the result of years of cultivation of the plant to provide an ideal habitat for red grouse, which is a game bird. Since the grouse needs young nutritious heather for feeding and older heather for cover and nesting, selective burning of the plant takes place every spring. As you walk along past the heather you will undoubtedly be told from time to time to "gobak, gobak, gobak" as you disturb

Continued on page 90

Route 16

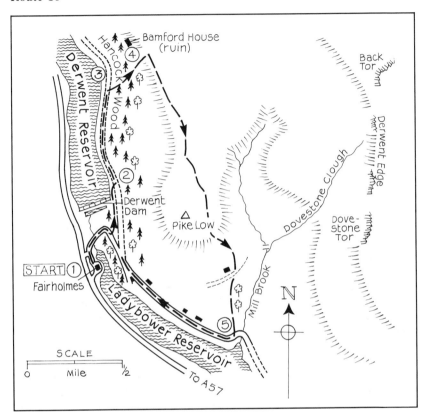

Whinchat. Brownish, streaked darker above, underparts buff. White eyestripe in cock.
White chin and wing patch. Black bill and legs

Route 16

Hancock Wood and Pike Low   4 miles

Start

At Fairholmes car park in the Derwent Valley. Turn north off the A57 on the west side of the Ashopton Viaduct along the road signposted to Derwent. Continue to a roundabout, the car park is next to it (GR 173893).

Route

1. *On leaving the car park walk past the Information Centre, then turn right along the road that passes below the Derwent Dam. Immediately after the road turns away from the dam, turn left along a footpath up through trees. Follow this up to the eastern end of the dam wall. Continue along a footpath with the reservoir wall on your left. Follow it to a track.*

2. *Turn left at the track and follow this alongside the Derwent Reservoir for just over ½ mile to where a steep, wooded valley joins on the right (Public Footpath sign to Bradfield and Strines).*

3. *Turn right here and follow the path up through the wood. On emerging from the wood, the footpath soon starts to wind its way up the very steep hillside, eventually to reach a junction with another footpath. (The ruins of Bamford House are just down to the left from here.)*

4. *Turn right and follow a more gradually ascending path as signposted for Pike Low and Derwent. Keep straight on this, following the waymarked route and ignoring any other possibilities. The path begins to descend after about ½ mile of walking on the level. A stiled fotpath leads downhill past a building owned by the National Trust. Follow it to the road that runs along the east side of Ladybower. (The ruins of Derwent village lie submerged just south of the point where the footpath joins the road.)*

5. *Turn right and follow the road back to the car park.*
the grouse as they graze. You might also spot a mountain hare in this area or, if you are very lucky, a golden plover.

From the highest point on the walk, near the summit of Pike Low, there are fine views both east towards Derwent Edge and south over the reservoirs. Pike Low, at 1329 feet above sea level, and the highest point on this stretch of moor, is a Bronze Age barrow. Obviously, Bronze Age people liked to bury their dead in high places. The term 'low', or 'hlaw' is a Saxon word that means a heaped structure and usually refers to a burial mound.

After descending from the moor, the footpath joins the lane that runs alongside Ladybower just north of the site of the submerged ruins of Derwent village. When the water level is low, which has occurred with greater frequency over the last two decades, the ruins of Derwent Hall and church can be seen.

The last mile is an easy stroll along a tarmac lane along which only anglers and residents may drive and cyclists ride. For those who are tired and thirsty, both hot and cold refreshments await at the shop adjacent to the Information Centre.

Refreshments
At Fairholmes — Shop selling hot and cold drinks and other refreshments.

Access by bus
To Fairholmes from Chesterfield, Sheffield and Castleton every day (Chesterfield Transport — Countybus Service).

On the way up to Crook Hill with Ashopton Viaduct below

Useful information

Walks in order of difficulty

The walks are arranged into four categories according to distance, and within each category they are listed in order of difficulty. Difficulty is gauged on the basis of how strenuous the walks are compared with others in the same category, although as a general rule the shorter the walk, the easier it is.

Walks under 4 miles

Route 2 — Stanton Moor (Variation I) — 3 miles
Route 6 — Ashford, Monsal Trail and Monsal Head (Shorter variation A) — 3 miles
Route 14 — Cave Dale and Windy Knoll (Variation I) — 2½ miles
Route 14 — Cave Dale and Windy Knoll (Variation II) — 3½ miles
Route 12 — High Neb and Sheepwash Bank (Variation) — 3 miles
Route 15 — Crook Hill and Ladybower (Variation) — 2½ miles

Walks from 4 to 4¾ miles

Route 6 — Ashford, Monsal Trail and Monsal Head (Variation B — 4 miles
Route 3 — Calton Lees (Edensor Variation) — 4 miles
Route 5 — Manner's Wood and Wye Valley — 4½ miles
Route 1 — Clough Wood and Rowtor Rocks — 4½ miles
Route 7 — Baslow Edge (Variation) — 4½ miles
Route 11 — Hathersage Moor, Bole Hill and Derwent Edge — 4 miles
Route 9 — Sir William Hill and Eyam Edge — 4 miles
Route 13 — Bradwell Edge and Abney Moor — 4¾ miles
Route 16 — Hancock Wood and Pike Low — 4 miles

Walks from 5 to 5¾ miles

Route 8 — Three Edges from Curbar Gap — 5½ miles
Route 6 — Ashford, Monsal Trail and Monsal Head — 5 miles
Route 3 — Calton Lees — 5½ miles
Route 4 — Haddon Fields and Lathkill Dale (Variation) — 5 miles
Route 10 — Peter Dale from Tideswell — 5 miles
Route 7 — Baslow Edge — 5 miles
Route 14 — Cave Dale and Windy Knoll — 5 miles
Route 4 — Haddon Fields and Lathkill Dale — 5¾ miles

Walks of 6 or more miles

Route 10 — Peter Dale from Tideswell (Variation) — 7 miles
Route 15 — Crook Hill and Ladybower — 7½ miles
Route 2 — Stanton Moor (Variation II) — 6 miles
Route 2 — Stanton Moor — 7¼ miles
Route 11 — Hathersage Moor, Bole Hill and Derwent Valley — 6 miles
Route 9 — Sir William Hill and Eyam Edge (Variation) — 7 miles
Route 12 — High Neb and Sheepwash Bank — 6 miles

Bus operators

Andrews of Tideswell. Tel. Buxton (0298) 871222.
Chesterfield Transport. Tel. Chesterfield (0246) 276666.
East Midland Motor Services. Tel. Chesterfield (0246) 211007.
Hulleys of Baslow. Tel. Baslow (0246) 582246.
PMT (Potteries Motor Traction). Tel. Stoke (0782) 747000.

SYS (South Yorkshire Transport). Tel. Sheffield (0742) 755655.
Trent Buses. Tel. Buxton (0298) 23098 or Derby (0332) 29220.
Whites World Travel. Tel. Hope Valley (0433) 630401.

Cycle hire centres

Ashbourne Mapleton Road. Tel. Ashbourne 43156.
Tissington the building adjacent to the village pond. Tel. Parwich 244.
Middleton Top 4½ miles south of Matlock half way between Middleton and Wirksworth off the B5023, at a picnic site on the High Peak Trail. Tel. Wirksworth 3204.
Hartington 2 The Market Place. Tel. Hartington 459 or Ashbourne 42629.
Parsley Hay 2 miles south of Monyash and just off the A515 Buxton to Ashbourne, at a picnic site on the High Peak Trail. Tel. Hartington 493.
Monsal Head adjacent to the Monsal Head Hotel on the B6465 1½ miles N.W. of Ashford-in-the-Water. Tel. Gt. Longstone 505 or Tideswell 871679.
Derwent Fairholmes Picnic Site, below the Derwent Dam, 2 miles north of Ashopton Viaduct (A57-Snake Pass). Tel. 0433-51261.
Waterhouses Waterhouses Station Car Park. Situated near the southern end of the Manifold Track. Tel. 05386-609.
Hayfield Hayfield Station Picnic Site on the Sett Valley Trail, just off the A624 Chapel to Glossop road. Tel. 0663-46222.
Bollington By the Peak and Plains Discovery Centre, Grimshaw Lane, Bollington, on the Middlewood Way and Cheshire Cycle Way. Tel. 0625-72681.

Nature trails

Black Rocks Trail ½ mile south of Cromford off the B5036, and starting at the Black Rocks Picnic Area.
Errwood Hall Trail Goyt Valley. Turn off the A5002 2 miles N.W. of Buxton. The trail starts at a Picnic Area.
Ilam Nature Trail in the grounds of Ilam Hall, Ilam. Tideswell Dale Trail — starts at a Picnic Area 1 mile south of Tideswell.
Padley and Longshaw Nature Trail starts at Longshaw Lodge, just off the A625 between Sheffield and Hathersage.
Sett Valley Trail starts at Hayfield Station Picnic site, just off the A624 Chapel to Glossop road.

Country parks and wildlife attractions

Alton Towers near Ashbourne. Leisure Park and Gardens, open April to October. Tel. Oakamoor 702458/702449.
Buxton Country Park Woodland walks and interpretation centre. Tel. Buxton 6978.
Chatsworth Farm and Adventure Playground The farm is designed with children in mind, and the adventure playground is superbly constructed. Open Easter to October. Tel. Baslow 2242.
Chestnut Centre Castleton Road, Chapel-en-le-Frith. Conservation Park, otter haven and owl sanctuary. Nature Trail. Visitor Centre, shop, refreshments. Open March to December daily, January and February on Saturdays and Sundays. Tel. (0298) 814099.
Gulliver's Kingdom, Matlock Bath Model Village and adventure playground. Open daily. Tel. Matlock 55970.
Ilam Country Park 4½ miles N.W. of Ashbourne. Park and woodland in Manifold Valley. Information Centre with exhibition on South Peak Estate. Open March to October, daily and weekends except Christmas October to March. (National Trust).
Longshaw Estate 3 miles S.E. of Hathersage. An area of moorland and woodland with lots of scope for walks of varying lengths and good for picnicking. Information Centre, shop and cafe at Longshaw Lodge. (National Trust).

Lyme Park National Trust Country Park, Disley A deer park centred on Lyme Hall, with adventure playground.
Riber Castle Wildlife Park near Matlock. British and European birds and animals, vintage car and motorcycle collection, children's playground and model railway. Tel. Matlock 2073.
The Torrs Riverside Park New Mills. Centred on a spectacular gorge at the confluence of the Goyt and Sett. Industrial relics, picnic sites. Heritage Centre and Information Centre, shop, teas and light refreshments. Tel. (0663) 746904.

Historic buildings

Chatsworth House Home of the Duke of Devonshire, open April to October. Tel. Baslow 2242.
Eyam Hall Eyam. 17th century manor house built and occupied by the Wright family. Open March 29 to October 31, Wednesday, Thursday, Sunday. Shop and refreshments. Tel. (0433) 631976.
Haddon Hall near Bakewell. The Duke of Rutland's medieval hall. Open April to September, Tuesday to Sunday (July and August, Tuesday to Saturday) Refreshments. Tel. (0629) 812855.
Peveril Castle Castleton. Impressive, ruined Norman castle with keep. Splendid views over Castleton. Open daily all year. Tel. Hope Valley 20613.
Winster Market Hall Winster. Late 17th or early 18th century stone market hall. Information Centre. (National Trust).

Museums

Aquarium and Waxworks Museum Matlock Bath. Tel. Matlock 3624.
Buxton Micrarium Nature seen through microscopes. Open April to November. Tel. Buxton 78662.
Buxton Museum Archaeological relics of the Peak District. Closed on Mondays. Tel. Buxton 4658.
Blue John Museum Castleton. Ollerenshaw Collection. One of the largest collections of Blue John in the world. Open daily except Christmas Day. Tel. (0433) 620642.
Carriage Museum Red House Stables, Old Road, Darley Dale. Over 40 horse-drawn carriages. Working stables. Scenic tours by coach and Four-in-Hand and short carriage rides by arrangement. Open all year. Tel. (0629) 733583.
Castleton Village Museum Methodist School Hall, Buxton Road. Local history, and geology. Wheelwright and blacksmith workshops. Open May to October, Sundays; June and July, Wednesdays; August, Tuesday to Thursday and weekends.
Longnor Folk Museum Exhibits and spinning demonstrations. Open Saturdays and Bank Holidays from Spring Bank Holiday weekend to end of first week in September.
National Stone Centre Porter Lane, Wirksworth. Story of stone from prehistoric axe factories to modern processing. Displays on geology, history technology and environment. Trails round fossil limestone reefs and quarries. Gem panning. Shop, refreshments. Open all year, daily. Tel. (0629) 824833/825403.
National Tramway Museum Crich, Matlock. Impressive museum with lots of exhibits, tram rides, period street, etc. Open April to October. Tel. (0773) 852565.
Old House Museum Bakewell. Tudor house and folk museum. Open daily, Easter to October. Tel. Bakewell 3647.
Peak District Mining Museum Matlock Bath. Exhibits and displays illustrating 2000 years of lead mining in the Peak District. Climbing shaft between floors for children. Open daily all year. Tel. Matlock 3834.
Temple Mine Matlock Bath. Working lead and fluorspar mine reconstructed as typical early 20th century workings. Open Easter to October, daily. Tel. (0629) 583834.

Industrial Archaeology

Caudwell's Mill and Craft Centre Rowsley, south of Bakewell. A working, water-powered flour mill. Craft workshops in Old Stable Courtyard. Craft shop, gallery, cafe. Open most of the year. Tel. (0629) 734374.

Cromford Mill Cromford. Sir Richard Arkwright's water-powered cotton spinning mill. Exhibition, slide show. Shops. Wholefood restaurant. Open daily, except Christmas Day. Tel. (0629) 824297.

High Peak Junction Workshops High Peak Junction, near Cromford. Original workshops of the Cromford and High Peak Railway. Railway exhibition, Information Centre, shop, canalside picnic area. Open Sundays throughout the winter period and daily April to October.

Leawood Pumphouse Cromford. Restored 19th century beam engine originally used to maintain water levels in the Cromford Canal. Car park at Lea. Open most weekends in summer. Tel. (0629) 823204/822831.

Magpie Mine Sheldon, 3 miles west of Bakewell. Remains of lead mine including chimneys, engine house and winding gear. Information about access from Peak District Mining Museum, Matlock Bath. Tel. (0629) 3834.

Middleton Top Engine House 2 miles S.W. of Cromford. Winding engine of former Cromford and High Peak Railway. Open Sundays and first Saturday of each month, when the engine is in steam. Tel. Wirksworth 3204.

Temple Mine Matlock Bath. Working lead and fluorspar mine reconstructed as typical early 20th century workings. Open Easter to October daily.

Show Caves and Mines

Bagshaw Cavern, Bradwell Limestone show cave, open daily, but by appointment only from October to Easter. Tel. Hope Valley 20540.

Blue John Cavern, Castleton Limestone show cave, open daily all year. Tel. Hope Valley 20638.

Good Luck Mine via Gellia, near Cromford. A working example of a mid-18th century lead mine. Open on first Sunday of each month, or by appointment. Tel. Chesterfield 72375.

Great Masson Cavern Heights of Abraham, Matlock Bath. Limestone show cave, open Sundays and Bank Holidays from Easter to October and daily during August. Tel. Matlock 2365.

Great Rutland Cavern and Nestus Mine Heights of Abraham, Matlock Bath. Limestone show cave, within which is a 17th century lead mine. Open daily from Easter to October. Tel. Matlock 2365.

Holme Bank Chert Mine, Bakewell Limestone show cave, open Easter to October. Tel. Darley Dale 4658.

Peak Cavern, Castleton Limestone show cave, open April to September. Tel. Hope Valley 20285.

Poole's Cavern, Buxton Country Park Limestone show cave, open Easter to October. Tel. Buxton 6978.

Speedwell Cavern, Castleton Limestone cave with underground boat ride, open daily all year. Tel. Hope Valley 20512.

Temple Mine, Matlock Bath Fluorite and lead mine, open daily all year. Tel. Matlock 3834.

Treak Cliff Cavern, Castleton Limestone show cave with fine grottoes, and veins of Blue John stone. Open daily all year. Tel. Hope Valley 20571.

Swimming pools

There are indoor pools at Ashbourne, Buxton, Leek and Matlock, and Hathersage has an outdoor heated swimming pool.

Market days

Bakewell — Monday
Buxton — Tuesday and Saturday
Chapel-en-le-Frith — Thursday
Chesterfield — Monday, Friday and Saturday
Glossop — Friday and Saturday
Leek — Wednesday
Macclesfield — Tuesday, Friday and Saturday
Matlock — Tuesday and Saturday
New Mills — Friday and Saturday
Wirksworth — Tuesday

Tourist Information Centres

Ashbourne 13 Market Place. Tel. (0335) 43666.
Bakewell Old Market Hall, Bridge Street. Tel. (0629) 813227.
Buxton The Crescent. Tel. (0298) 25106.
Castleton Castle Street. Tel. (0433) 620679.
Edale. Tel. (0433) 670207.
Glossop The Gatehouse, Victoria Street. Tel. (0457) 855920.
Hayfield Old Station Yard. Tel. (0663) 46222.
Leek 1 Market Place. Tel. (0538) 381000.
Macclesfield Town Hall, Market Place. Tel. (0625) 21955.
Matlock Bath The Pavilion. Tel. (0629) 55082.
New Mills Heritage Centre. Tel. (0663) 746904.

Recommended reading

Countryside Commission. *Out in the Country, Where You Can Go and What You Can Do* (includes the Countryside Access Charter). Countryside Commission, Cheltenham, 1985.
Porter, L. *The Visitor's Guide to the Peak District.* Moorland Publishing, Ashbourne, 1989.
Robson, L. *A Gazetteer of the White Peak.* J.H. Hall & Sons, Derby, 1991.
Smith, R. *The Peak National Park. Countryside Commission Official Guide.* Webb & Bower, Exeter, 1987.

THE FAMILY WALKS SERIES

Family Walks on Anglesey. Laurence Main. ISBN 0 907758 665.

Family Walks in Berkshire & North Hampshire. Kathy Sharp. ISBN 0 907758 371

Family Walks around Bristol, Bath & the Mendips. Nigel Vile. ISBN 0 907758 193.

Family Walks around Cardiff & the Valleys. Gordon Hindess. ISBN 0 907758 541.

Family Walks in Cheshire. Chris Buckland. ISBN 0 907758 290.

Family Walks in Cornwall. John Caswell. ISBN 0 907758 55X.

Family Walks in the Cotswolds. Gordon Ottewell. ISBN 0 907758 150

Family Walks on Exmoor & the Quantocks. John Caswell. ISBN 0 907758 460.

Family Walks in South Gloucestershire. Gordon Ottewell. ISBN 0 907758 399.

Family Walks in Gower. Amanda Green. ISBN 0 907758 630.

Family Walks in Hereford and Worcester. Gordon Ottewell. ISBN 0 907758 207.

Family Walks on the Isle of Wight. Laurence Main. ISBN 0 907758 568.

Family Walks in North West Kent. Clive Cutter. ISBN 0 907758 363.

Family Walks in the Lake District. Barry McKay, ISBN 0 907758 401.

Family Walks in Mendip, Avalon & Sedgemoor. Nigel Vile. ISBN 0 907758 41X.

Family Walks in the New Forest. Nigel Vile. ISBN 0 907758 606.

Family Walks in Oxfordshire. Laurence Main. ISBN 0 907758 38X.

Family Walks in the Dark Peak. Norman Taylor. ISBN 0 907758 169.

Family Walks in the White Peak. Norman Taylor. ISBN 0 907758 096.

Family Walks in South Derbyshire. Gordon Ottewell. ISBN 0 907758 614.

Family Walks in South Shropshire. Marian Newton. ISBN 0 907758 304.

Family Walks in Snowdonia. Laurence Main. ISBN 0 907758 320.

Family Walks in the Staffordshire Peaks and Potteries. Les Lumsdon. ISBN 0 907758 347.

Family Walks around Stratford & Banbury. Gordon Ottewell. ISBN 0 907758 495.

Family Walks in Suffolk. C.J. Francis. ISBN 0 907758 649.

Family Walks around Swansea. Raymond Humphreys. ISBN 0 907758 622.

Family Walks in the Teme Valley. Camilla Harrison. ISBN 0 907758 452.

Family Walks in Three Peaks & Malham. Howard Beck. ISBN 0 907758 428.

Family Walks in Mid Wales. Laurence Main. ISBN 0 907758 274.

Family Walks in the North Wales Borderlands. Gordon Emery. ISBN 0 907758 5909.

Family Walks in Warwickshire. Geoff Allen. ISBN 0 907758 533.

Family Walks in the Weald of Kent & Sussex. Clive Cutter. ISBN 0 907758 517.

Family Walks in Wiltshire. Nigel Vile. ISBN 0 907758 215.

Family Walks in the Wye Valley. Heather & Jon Hurley. ISBN 0 907758 266.

Family Walks in the North Yorkshire Dales. Howard Beck. ISBN 0 907758 525.

Family Walks in South Yorkshire. Norman Taylor. ISBN 0 907758 258.

Family Walks in West Yorkshire. Howard Beck. ISBN 0 907758 436.

The publishers welcome suggestions for further titles in this series; and will be pleased to consider manuscripts relating to Derbyshire from new or established authors.

Scarthin Books of Cromford, in the Peak District, are also leading second-hand and antiquarian booksellers, and are eager to purchase specialised material, both ancient and modern.

Contact Dr D.J. Mitchell, 0629-823272.